THE LUFTWAFFE

TIME
LIFE ®
BOOKS

Other Publications:

PLANET EARTH
COLLECTOR'S LIBRARY OF THE CIVIL WAR
LIBRARY OF HEALTH
CLASSICS OF THE OLD WEST
THE GOOD COOK
THE SEAFARERS
THE ENCYCLOPEDIA OF COLLECTIBLES
THE GREAT CITIES
WORLD WAR II
HOME REPAIR AND IMPROVEMENT
THE WORLD'S WILD PLACES
THE TIME-LIFE LIBRARY OF BOATING
HUMAN BEHAVIOR
THE ART OF SEWING
THE OLD WEST
THE EMERGENCE OF MAN
THE AMERICAN WILDERNESS
THE TIME-LIFE ENCYCLOPEDIA OF GARDENING
LIFE LIBRARY OF PHOTOGRAPHY
THIS FABULOUS CENTURY
FOODS OF THE WORLD
TIME-LIFE LIBRARY OF AMERICA
TIME-LIFE LIBRARY OF ART
GREAT AGES OF MAN
LIFE SCIENCE LIBRARY
THE LIFE HISTORY OF THE UNITED STATES
TIME READING PROGRAM
LIFE NATURE LIBRARY
LIFE WORLD LIBRARY

FAMILY LIBRARY:
HOW THINGS WORK IN YOUR HOME
THE TIME-LIFE BOOK OF THE FAMILY CAR
THE TIME-LIFE FAMILY LEGAL GUIDE
THE TIME-LIFE BOOK OF FAMILY FINANCE

This volume is one of a series that traces the adventure and science of aviation, from the earliest manned balloon ascension through the era of jet flight.

THE LUFTWAFFE

BY THE EDITORS OF TIME-LIFE BOOKS

THE EPIC OF FLIGHT

TIME-LIFE BOOKS, ALEXANDRIA, VIRGINIA

THE EPIC OF FLIGHT

EDITOR: Dale M. Brown
Senior Editor: Jim Hicks
Designer: Raymond Ripper
Chief Researcher: W. Mark Hamilton

Editorial Staff for *The Luftwaffe*
Picture Editor: Marion F. Briggs
Text Editors: David S. Thomson, Russell B. Adams Jr.
Writers: Kevin D. Armstrong, Robert A. Doyle,
Laura Longley, Glenn Martin McNatt
Researchers: LaVerle Berry, Patricia A. Cassidy (principals),
Betty Ajemian, Roxie France, Adrienne George, Elizabeth L.
Parker, Jules Taylor, Maria Zacharias
Assistant Designer: Van W. Carney
Copy Coordinators: Elizabeth Graham, Anthony K. Pordes
Picture Coordinator: Betsy Donahue
Editorial Assistant: Caroline A. Boubin

Special Contributors: Derek Dempster,
Katie Hooper McGregor, Herbert Molloy Mason Jr.,
John Neary, Nancy Cromwell Scott

Editorial Operations
Production Director: Feliciano Madrid
  Assistants: Peter A. Inchauteguiz, Karen A. Meyerson
Copy Processing: Gordon E. Buck
Quality Control Director: Robert L. Young
  Assistant: James J. Cox
  Associates: Daniel J. McSweeney, Michael G. Wight
Art Coordinator: Anne B. Landry
Copy Room Director: Susan Galloway Goldberg
  Assistants: Celia Beattie, Ricki Tarlow

Correspondents: Elisabeth Kraemer (Bonn); Margot
Hapgood, Dorothy Bacon (London); Susan Jonas, Lucy T.
Voulgaris (New York); Maria Vincenza Aloisi, Josephine du
Brusle (Paris); Ann Natanson (Rome). Valuable assistance
was also provided by: Helga Kohl (Bonn); Judy Aspinall,
Millicent Trowbridge (London); Christina Lieberman, Tina
Voulgaris (New York); Traudl Lessing (Vienna); Bodgan
Turek (Warsaw).

THE CONSULTANTS *for The Luftwaffe*
Dr. Edward L. Homze, the principal consultant, was appointed Professor of History at the University of Nebraska at Lincoln in 1965. A former United States Air Force bombardier-navigator in B-47 jets, he has written many books and articles on Germany, including *Arming the Luftwaffe* and *Foreign Labor in Nazi Germany.*

Dr. Horst Boog was named a Director of the Office of Military History in Freiburg, West Germany, in 1980. He has written several studies of the Luftwaffe, among them *Command and Leadership of the German Luftwaffe: 1935-1945.*

THE CONSULTANTS *for The Epic of Flight*
Charles Harvard Gibbs-Smith was Research Fellow at the Science Museum, London, and a Keeper-Emeritus of the Victoria and Albert Museum, London. He wrote or edited some 20 books and numerous articles on aeronautical history. In 1978 he was the first Lindbergh Professor of Aerospace History at the National Air and Space Museum, Smithsonian Institution, Washington.

Dr. Hidemasa Kimura, honorary professor at Nippon University, Tokyo, is the author of numerous books on the history of aviation and is a widely known authority on aeronautical engineering and aircraft design. One plane that he designed established a world distance record in 1938.

For information about any Time-Life book, please write:
Reader Information
Time-Life Books
541 North Fairbanks Court
Chicago, Illinois 60611

Library of Congress Cataloguing in Publication Data
  Luftwaffe.
  (Epic of flight)
  Bibliography: p.
  Includes index.
  1. World War, 1939-1945—Aerial operations, German.
2. Germany. Luftwaffe—History—World War, 1939-1945.
I. Time-Life Books. II. Series.
D787.L82   940.54'4943   81-21486
ISBN 0-8094-3339-7   AACR2
ISBN 0-8094-3337-0 (retail ed.)
ISBN 0-8094-3338-9 (lib. bdg.)
ISBN 0-8094-3340-0 (deluxe ed.)

CONTENTS

Forging the world's mightiest air force

In March 1935, only two years after he came to power in Germany, Adolf Hitler openly defied the Treaty of Versailles imposed on his country at the end of World War I and announced a massive program of rearmament. The plan called for a *Reichsluftwaffe,* a national air force whose squadrons, as Nazi propagandists said, would put a "steel roof over Germany" and "darken out the sun."

At the time, the nation's frontline air strength amounted to a mere three squadrons of fighters and five of bombers—all forbidden under the Treaty. But Hitler missed no opportunity to endow his nascent air arm with an aura of pride and power. In carefully arranged ceremonies, he gave Luftwaffe units names redolent of past glories; the first such event *(right)* took place on March 14, 1935, when he dubbed a fighter squadron *Jagdgeschwader Richthofen* after Germany's top World War I ace. And during the gaudy displays of military might staged at Nuremberg each year after that, he saw to it that squadrons of planes blazoned with black crosses thundered overhead.

The chief purpose of these spectacles was simply to awe other countries, but the Luftwaffe was in fact becoming a mighty force. Its commander, Hermann Göring, with vital aid from his efficient production chief Erhard Milch, performed prodigies to make the Reich's air fleets truly potent. The output of Germany's aircraft industry shot upward from a few hundred planes a year to thousands. Simultaneously, new combat machines replaced obsolete models, until virtually all of the Luftwaffe's fighters and bombers were swift monoplanes of all-metal construction. By 1939, when Hitler set into motion his schemes for European conquest, the Luftwaffe boasted more than 4,000 frontline combat aircraft, making it the most formidable air force in the world.

Hitler and Göring lead a group of officers, including Luftwaffe production boss Erhard Milch (fourth from left), past the planes of the newly christened Richthofen squadron in 1935. The biplane Heinkel 51s and Arado 65s were soon replaced by superior single-wing aircraft.

Student pilots snap to attention in front of a primary trainer in 1935. Prewar Luftwaffe flying schools gave trainees 250 hours of flying time during a rigorous course of instruction that lasted two years.

Pilots race to their Heinkel 51 fighters during a training exercise in August 1935, shortly after the Luftwaffe ceased to be a clandestine force.

Fuselage sections of Junkers 87B dive bombers crowd the floor of an aircraft plant just before the War; 557 Ju 87s were produced in 1939.

Workers in 1939 complete assembly of a pair of Heinkel 111 medium bombers that already bear wartime markings. Conceived in 1934 to fulfill the dual role of bomber and airliner, the He 111 first saw military action during the 1936-1939 Spanish Civil War.

Trailing ribbons of smoke, slim, fast Dornier 17 twin-engined bombers roar over the 1938 Nuremberg Rally. Antiaircraft guns in the foreground fire blank shells at the planes as a vast crowd watches from the flag-bedecked grandstand built for the annual shows of German military power.

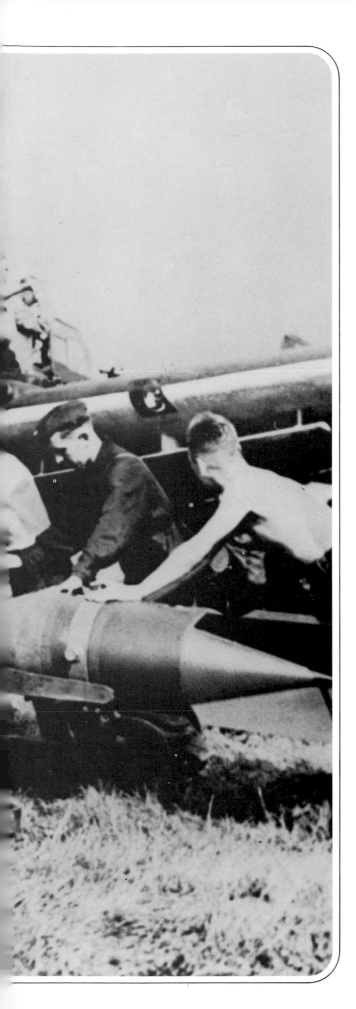

1

A blitzkrieg from the sky

Only very courageous—or foolhardy—pilots would have dared to fly through the curtains of fog and mist that blanketed the undulating lands along the frontier between northeastern Germany and Poland at daybreak on September 1, 1939. Luftwaffe First Lieutenant Bruno Dilley, a former policeman, had courage in abundance, and he decided to go ahead with the mission he was assigned to lead, despite the atrocious flying weather. He and his wingmen, Second Lieutenant Horst Schiller and Sergeant Gerhard Grenzel, were all thoroughly trained fliers, and they would be piloting rugged and agile planes—Junkers 87 dive bombers, called Stukas. Their mission was of vital tactical importance to the German Army, poised to plunge into Poland that very morning to strike the first blow of World War II.

Dilley's objective was a pair of huge steel railroad bridges that spanned the Vistula River on the edge of the town of Dirschau. The Stukas were not to demolish the bridges, however; the High Command of the German Army wanted the twin spans intact so that German troops and supplies could speed across the Vistula in their intended *Blitzkrieg,* or lightning war, against the Polish Army. Dilley's task was to prevent the Poles themselves from blowing the bridges as a defensive measure. Polish Army engineers had already affixed explosive charges to the bridge structures; the three Luftwaffe pilots were to destroy the wires that connected the explosives with remote electrical detonators located within the Dirschau railroad station.

Severing slender wires with bombs dropped from planes flying at high speed was a difficult undertaking, to say the least. To increase their chances of success, Dilley and his wingmen had scouted the area, changing into civilian clothes and boarding the Berlin-Königsberg express, which ran through a slim corridor of Poland between Germany and East Prussia and across the vital Vistula bridges. From the train the German airmen had seen the detonator wires for themselves: They were strung along the riverbank. To hit so small a target, the Stukas—normally used as dive bombers—would have to be flown horizontally at treetop level. It was a risky business at best, and the fog and mist on the morning of September 1 made it many times more hazardous.

Beneath the ominous snout of a Junkers 87 Stuka dive bomber, a Luftwaffe ground crew delivers the warplane's first complement of bombs for the following day's blitzkrieg into Polish territory.

At 4:26 a.m., Dilley, Schiller and Grenzel gunned their Stukas across a rough airfield near Elbing, East Prussia, and took off. Dirschau lay 24 miles away. If all went well, they would reach it in just eight minutes.

For six minutes the three pilots and the rear gunners sitting behind them in the Stukas' two-seat cockpits hurtled straight ahead through blinding scud, the planes' big 1,210-horsepower Jumo 211D engines roaring at full throttle. Even a small error in calculating altitude would have meant smashing into one of the borderland's rolling hills, and each Stuka carried a 550-pound bomb under its fuselage and four 110-pounders below the wings that would have made any contact with the ground instantly fatal.

Two minutes from the target, Dilley dimly perceived the silver gray water of the Vistula beneath his wings. He banked to turn downstream toward the bridges, his wingmen following in line-astern formation. All three skimmed along less than 100 feet above the river.

The moment he sighted the bridges glimmering through the mist, Dilley radioed his pilots, "target ahead," and eased his Stuka into line with the embankment to the left of the two spans. He pressed the bomb-release button on his control stick when his plane was barely 100 yards from the twin spans' girders, then jerked the stick back and to the left. The Stuka, relieved of its bombs, leaped over the bridges in a tight climbing turn to port. Schiller followed in carbon-copy style. So did Grenzel. As they swung away, they could see that their bombs had plastered the area where the wires were strung. The time was 4:34 a.m., 11 minutes before the Army's scheduled 4:45 attack. With whoops of joy, they streaked back toward the East Prussian border and their base.

Although their mission turned out to be only a partial success—the Poles reconnected some of the wires and blew one span—Dilley and his wingmen had convincingly demonstrated the expertise and nerve that would characterize the pilots of Germany's air force, the Luftwaffe, throughout World War II. *Luftwaffe* translates simply as "air weapon," but it came to mean something more powerful and dangerous than those bland syllables imply.

To the airmen who faced Germany's aerial weapon—those of Poland first, then of France and Britain's RAF, and later those of the Soviet Union and the United States—the word Luftwaffe connoted desperate battles against an extraordinarily tenacious and resourceful foe. To the ground armies and the peoples of Poland, Belgium, Holland, France, Britain and the Soviet Union, it meant slashing attacks that almost magically cleared the way for the gray-clad German Army that overran most of Europe. In the first years of the conflict, the Luftwaffe seemed both omnipresent and nearly invincible as it fought on fronts as distant as North Africa and northern Russia. It was in fact the world's finest air force at the time, with air crews that combined great ability and superb morale. Even later, when the fortunes of war were reversed, the Luftwaffe defied the mightiest Allied efforts to knock it from the skies.

The invasion of Poland begun by Bruno Dilley and his squadron-

First Lieutenant Bruno Dilley, who led the first air strike of World War II, smiles down from the cockpit of his Stuka. Dilley typified the hard use the Reich made of its pilots: In the course of the War he flew nearly 650 missions and was shot down four times, twice behind enemy lines.

Poles from Dirschau are pressed into service clearing wreckage from a railroad bridge blown into the Vistula River by retreating Polish Army engineers. Precision bombing raids by Bruno Dilley and his wingmen prevented the Poles from demolishing the span in the background.

mates had long been the ambition of Germany's *Führer* (leader), Adolf Hitler, and of some of the Reich's military planners. They were determined to regain territory that they believed had been unfairly confiscated under the terms of the Treaty of Versailles, the punitive pact forced upon Germany after its defeat in World War I. No territorial provision of the Treaty rankled the Germans more than the one giving Poland a 50-mile-wide corridor to the Baltic Sea; this clause isolated Germany's easternmost province of East Prussia and put the old German seaport of Danzig (today's Gdansk) under League of Nations' supervision and Polish economic control.

In addition to regaining what had been lost, Hitler was obsessed with acquiring *Lebensraum*—additional "living space"—in the East for Germany's 80 million people. If he could not extend Germany's borders peacefully, he was determined to use force.

Until 1939, the Führer had managed to expand German rule without firing a shot. His troops had marched into the Rhineland in 1936, defying the Versailles Treaty, which had specified that this border area between France and Germany must remain demilitarized. By threat, he succeeded in annexing Austria in March 1938. Next, partly by boasting of the Luftwaffe's power at the Munich Conference in September 1938, he bullied France and Britain into letting his troops occupy a portion of Czechoslovakia; having bitten off a chunk of that unfortunate nation, Hitler swiftly swallowed the rest.

After such a string of coups, it was only a matter of time before the Führer called upon the Poles to hand over Danzig, or else—and secretly began planning the conquest of the entire country. He faced one big problem: Britain and France were pledged to declare war if the Wehrmacht, Germany's armed forces, violated the Polish border. But Hitler was convinced that the Western powers, having supinely let him have

Austria and Czechoslovakia, would again back down. And even if they did declare war, he expected them to have a change of heart after they realized the true strength of his military machine. In either case, he was determined to make Poland the next addition to his Greater Germany.

As a prelude to invasion, the Führer and his propagandists trumpeted charges that people of German origin living within Poland were being brutalized by ''bestial'' Poles and that the Polish Army was systematically sending raiding parties across the border into Germany. ''The Polish state has refused the peaceful settlement of relations which I desired,'' Hitler ranted on the morning the conflict began, ''and has appealed to arms. A series of violations of the frontier, intolerable to a great power, proves that Poland is no longer willing to respect the frontier of the Reich. In order to put an end to this lunacy, I have no other choice than to meet force with force from now on!'' Few outside Germany were taken in by such shameless mendacity, but to Hitler this mattered little. He had the weapons: 44 Army divisions—about 1,500,000 men—poised on Poland's long, hard-to-defend frontier, and two air fleets, totaling almost 1,600 Luftwaffe planes, ready to spearhead that massive force's thrusts.

Bruno Dilley's raid—a pinpoint attack in support of Wehrmacht operations—foreshadowed the Luftwaffe's primary role in the War it began. The German air force and its planes were designed for assaults on military targets, preparing the way for the Army's advancing tanks and infantry. Dilley's Stuka epitomized this theory of how air power should be employed. A small, single-engined plane with a maximum bomb-load of only 1,000 pounds and a normal range of 370 miles, the Stuka was clearly not well suited for raids deep within an enemy's homeland, striking at factories and power plants. But screaming earthward in a power dive—the name Stuka was short for *Sturzkampfflugzeug,* or dive bomber—it could accurately plant bombs on an enemy troop concentration, a column of armored vehicles, an entrenched strong point or on any other obstacle that might frustrate the advancing German ground forces' freedom of movement.

The Luftwaffe's other bombers in 1939, the pencil-slim Dornier 17 and the glass-nosed Heinkel 111, were twin-engined aircraft with medium range and bomb-carrying capacity. They also were best suited for missions in support of the Army, such as shattering an enemy's railways and roads and thus paralyzing his supply system.

The job of the Luftwaffe's fighter planes—the fast and agile Messerschmitt 109 and its heavier brother, the Messerschmitt 110, a twin-engined fighter dubbed *Zerstörer,* or Destroyer—was to clear the skies of opposing aircraft so that the German bombers could roam unmolested over the front lines and into the enemy's rear areas.

The Luftwaffe had emerged as the spearhead for the Wehrmacht's armored columns chiefly because of the character and background of two men: Field Marshal Hermann Göring, who had served as a pilot in Germany's World War I air force, and Lieutenant General Wolfram von

General Alexander Löhr commanded a huge Luftwaffe air fleet that led the German thrust across Poland's border. A friend of Hermann Göring, Löhr was one of the few Austrians to hold positions of power in the Reich after Austria was annexed in 1938.

Richthofen, cousin of the legendary "Red Baron," Manfred von Richthofen, the most famous German ace of the Kaiser's war.

Göring, bitter over his country's defeat in 1918 and enraged by the severe strictures imposed on Germany by the Versailles Treaty, had joined Adolf Hitler's outcast National Socialist Party early in the 1920s, seeing it as Germany's best hope for rebirth—and revenge. When Hitler and the Nazis came to power in 1933, Göring was rewarded with the post of Air Minister, which included overall command of the nascent Luftwaffe. As a former freewheeling fighter commander, Göring was more attuned to the concept of tactical air power than he was to the theories of strategic air power—the dull, methodical pounding of an enemy's war industries—being preached during the 1920s and 1930s by Sir Hugh Trenchard, chief of the RAF, and by America's apostle of air power, General Billy Mitchell. Like most of Germany's military planners, he envisioned the Reich winning a series of short, sharp wars rather than becoming involved in a long-term, multifront conflict. For such limited struggles, bombers capable of ground-support missions would be sufficient—and long-range strategic bombers unnecessary.

Göring had another reason to favor small and medium bombers. Hitler, impatient to embark on his program of conquest, wanted the largest air force that could be built in a short length of time. One- and two-engined aircraft could be built far more rapidly and cheaply than complex four-engined bombers. So Göring canceled the further development of two big bombers that were ready for flight trials in 1936 and ordered Germany's fast-expanding aircraft industry to concentrate on turning out large numbers of He 111s and Do 17s, which were already in prototype or limited production. "The Führer will not ask how big the bombers are," Göring remarked at the time to one of his chief lieutenants, "but how many there are."

Wolfram von Richthofen was no less an enthusiast of tactical air power, having seen it work with devastating results in the Spanish Civil War. The eruption of that conflict in 1936 had been welcomed by Hitler and his generals as a heaven-sent opportunity for the young German air force to test its planes, train its air crews and develop new fighting techniques under modern battle conditions. Richthofen for a time commanded the Luftwaffe contingent, called the Condor Legion, that Hitler sent to aid the forces of General Francisco Franco.

In Spain, Richthofen found that a small biplane, the Heinkel 51, though obsolete as a fighter, made an effective low-level bomber and strafer, especially when armed with clusters of small, 22-pound incendiary bombs known as flambos. These incendiaries were first used by one of Richthofen's more innovative pilots, Lieutenant Adolf Galland, who would later become commander of all Luftwaffe fighters. The flambo, Galland noted long after World War II, was an "early prototype of the modern napalm bomb." It consisted of a can that was filled with a mixture of high-octane aviation fuel and motor oil and was connected to a fragmentation bomb. After routing Republican troops from their

Albert Kesselring also directed a Luftwaffe fleet that provided air support for the German ground forces that were heading toward Warsaw. Kesselring came to be regarded as one of the Führer's most formidable generals.

19

trenches with this deadly device, Galland and his nine-plane squadron would fly in a single file to machine-gun the infantrymen as they fled the streams of blazing gasoline that coursed through their positions.

Richthofen also discovered in Spain that the key to effective air-ground cooperation was close liaison between the local air commander and the officers commanding the ground forces in that sector of the front. With characteristic thoroughness, Richthofen would himself visit forward posts to ask the Spanish officers which enemy strong points needed to be bombed and strafed. He would then order his squadrons to hit those targets and would watch the results with field glasses.

The techniques and procedures that Richthofen worked out in Spain were regarded with some doubt back in Germany. He was nevertheless allowed to create a special air division that embodied his ideas of tactical air power. It had three dive-bomber wings of about 40 Stukas each, a ground-attack wing of 36 slow but heavily armored Henschel 123 biplanes, a similarly sized wing of twin-engined Me 110 fighters that could be converted into potent ground-attack aircraft and a reconnaissance squadron of some 10 Henschel parasol-winged observation planes.

When Germany unleashed its might against Poland on the morning of September 1, 1939, Richthofen was at the center of the action. The assignment of his air division was to punch holes in the Polish fortifications along the southern sector of the German-Polish border for General Walther von Reichenau's Tenth Army, the invasion vanguard of Army Group South. Richthofen and Reichenau shared quarters in Schönwald Castle, six miles from the Polish frontier.

Richthofen's air division made up about half of Luftflotte 4—Air Fleet 4—which was based in the regions of Wartaland, Silesia and Slovakia, facing Poland's southwestern border. Luftflotte 4 was commanded by General Alexander Löhr, an Austrian professional officer who had transferred to the Luftwaffe after his nation was absorbed by Germany in 1938. In the north, poised to strike from the Pomeranian plain of northeastern Germany and from East Prussia in support of the ground forces based there, was Luftflotte 1, which was commanded by General Albert Kesselring, a stocky and energetic veteran of World War I.

The Wehrmacht's plan for the campaign against Poland was a simple one. The 630,000 men of Army Group North, commanded by General Fedor von Bock, would thrust southward toward Warsaw. At the same time, Army Group South, containing 886,000 men and directed by General Gerd von Rundstedt, would drive northeastward from the Silesian region. Together, the two army groups—both with panzer (armored) divisions of tanks and motorized infantry in the lead—would envelop the main body of the Polish Army in a crushing embrace.

To carry out its part in the giant pincer movement, the Luftwaffe had mustered 648 He 111 and Do 17 bombers, 219 Stukas, 210 Me 110 heavy fighters and Me 109 single-engined fighters, 36 Henschel 123 ground-attack planes, and about 470 assorted reconnaissance and transport aircraft. The Polish Air Force was no match for this assem-

A P.37 Elk medium bomber, Poland's only up-to-date aircraft in 1939, is stationed by a row of gull-winged P.11 fighters at a field near Warsaw. The glass-nosed, twin-engined Elk had a top speed of 276 mph and could carry a 5,600-pound payload of bombs.

blage. When the Germans attacked, the Poles were caught with only about 400 frontline aircraft—some 160 fighters, 118 light bombers, 36 medium bombers and 85 reconnaissance planes.

Apart from the 36 Elk-type medium bombers, which were up-to-date twin-engined machines, the Polish aircraft were obsolescent or obsolete by 1939 standards. Most of the fighters were PZL P.11s made by Warsaw's Panstwowe Zaklady Lotnicze, or National Aviation Plants. They were high-wing monoplanes whose basic design dated back to 1931. Even at their optimum fighting altitude of 18,000 feet, the P.11s were almost 100 miles per hour slower than the German Me 109s and marginally slower than many of the German bombers. In addition, the P.11s were scantily armed: Many carried only two light machine guns.

But the Luftwaffe was taking no chances against its vastly overmatched foe. As a first order of business, the two German air fleets intended to smash the enemy's airfields and thus gain complete mastery of the air over the battlefront. Stukas, Heinkels, Dorniers and escorting fighters were being readied for the assignment even as Bruno Dilley and his wingmen headed back toward their East Prussian base.

Most of the planes taking off to hit the Polish airfields came from Löhr's Luftflotte 4 in the south. Up north the fog and mist that had nearly frustrated Dilley's raid plagued Kesselring's Luftflotte 1 until the first day of the War was almost half over. In the Silesian sector the weather was not ideal either; in fact, much of Poland that day was covered by banks of drifting cloud. But Löhr's planes could get off their runways, and the main body of the air fleet found a break in the weather over Cracow. They headed right for the ancient city's principal airfield.

First on the scene were 60 He 111 bombers of the 4th Bomber Group, which was based at Langenau, Silesia, 45 flying minutes away. Split into two waves and flying in tight formation, they approached the target at 12,000 feet, high enough to give the escorting Me 110s time to fend off any intercepting Polish fighters. But as the Heinkels dropped 48 tons of bombs on the target, the Poles failed to make an appearance. Next to bomb were some 30 Stukas, followed by about 100 Do 17 "Flying Pencils" to finish the job. By the time this last wave arrived, the Cracow airport's hangars were blazing, and its fuel depots were sending aloft thick columns of black smoke, obscuring the runways and other installations. So the leader of the Dorniers, Colonel Wolfgang von Stutterheim, ordered his planes to attack at treetop level. Screaming along at 240 miles an hour, the bombers hemstitched a line of craters down the main runway with 110-pound bombs. Before the Luftwaffe planes broke off this final attack, the Cracow airport was a ruin.

As the weather cleared, more Stukas, Heinkels and Dorniers pounded the airfields near half a dozen other Polish cities, one Heinkel group penetrating all the way to Lvov, 300 miles inside the Polish border, and there dropping 22 tons of bombs on hangars and runways.

While the airfields were under attack, additional Luftwaffe bombers were putting into effect another part of the Luftwaffe's plan of battle.

Ranging up and down the length of Poland, they pulverized the life lines of the Polish ground armies—the roads and railways along which enemy reinforcements and supplies would have to move. This tactic of isolating the battlefield would be a much-copied application of air power—highly effective in preventing a defending army from responding to the thrusts of an attacking army that possesses fast-moving tanks and motorized infantry. In the first Luftwaffe strikes against Polish behind-the-front communications, German bombers smashed rail junctions in key towns and cities such as Katowice, Lvov, Radom, Lublin, Vilna and Grodno, and then went on to obliterate smaller targets—crossroads, bridges and railroad tracks. Such attacks, which continued for the next several days, blasted the Poles' troop-movement system into hopeless disorder, making organized resistance all but impossible.

A German bomber-group commander, Major Erich Munske, recalled the effects of one such raid. Flying south out of the mist and cloud that initially frustrated most of Luftflotte 1's planned operations in the north, Munske saw the fog "disintegrate into veils and finally stop. There below were silver rails and a small red railroad station, with a locomotive steaming and the cars decorated with the branches of green shrubs. The

Scattering incendiaries like so many oversized matchsticks, a Heinkel 111 soars over a break in the clouds during a raid into Poland. The Luftwaffe used fire bombs to rout advancing columns of troops and, later, to incinerate the city of Warsaw.

people in the train—Polish reservists going toward the front—were waving their hats from the train windows; they thought we were friendly planes from the Polish Air Force. It was a strange feeling, dropping bombs on such unsuspecting people. The first bomb falls and it drops right on top of one of the railway cars. A fountain of smoke and ruin, people flying in all directions. More bombs hit their mark, too. Then a single antiaircraft gun shoots from below. It does not seem dangerous but, strangely, it is a relief to feel that the enemy is also shooting."

The carnage was not all on one side, however. On landing at his base, Munske found a crowd gathered around another returned bomber. "A man is being lifted from the cockpit. Many hands are raised to support the body. I go up to the plane and see that the control panel is completely smashed, apparently a direct hit. The glass is red with blood and bits of uniform and flesh are spattered about the cabin. On the ground next to the plane lies a body. It is Lieutenant Schott; antiaircraft fire tore him apart, but his face is serene and he looks as if he is sleeping."

While some Stuka squadrons and entire wings of 30 or more Henschels and Dorniers each were obliterating rail junctions, crossroads and airfields deep within Poland, Richthofen's Stukas and other aircraft were blasting away at the Polish Army's strong points and concentrations along the frontier. Just before sunrise on September 1, a key part of Richthofen's air division, the 36 Hs 123 biplanes, commanded by Major Werner Spielvogel, took off despite a high haze. The first squadron, led by Captain Otto Weiss, roared over Richthofen's forward command post toward its target, the Polish positions near the frontier village of Panki, opposite Army Group South's spearheading Tenth Army.

Taking the Poles by surprise, Weiss's planes dropped flambos—the primitive incendiary and fragmentation bombs first used in Spain by Galland. Everything they hit was enveloped in flame and smoke. Following hard on Weiss's heels was Galland himself, leading the second group of Henschels. As Galland and his men completed their attack, other planes wheeled in behind them to strafe the Poles, who were now starting to throw up fire from light antiaircraft guns and rifles.

From his forward command post barely three miles away, Richthofen and his staff, all veterans of Spain, watched fascinated as the Henschels dipped and rose, buzzed like hornets and provoked the Polish guns into intensified fire. Then, as suddenly as they had arrived, they were gone, forced by their limited range to return to their airfield to refuel.

Not enough calls were coming in from General von Reichenau's attacking troops to suit Richthofen's taste. He was certain there were more targets that his Henschels and Stukas should be hitting to prepare the way for the ground troops. He had learned in Spain that an air commander often had to see for himself what targets needed attention, since infantry and tank officers, in the heat of combat, frequently neglected to call for air support. So Richthofen climbed into his Fieseler observation plane, called a Stork because of its tall, thin landing gear, and took off from the level ground of a potato patch next to his command post.

Flying over the front, Richthofen spied a wealth of targets—Polish machine-gun nests and artillery that were stalling the German advance. He became so enthralled in his scouting, in fact, that he strayed beyond the enemy lines, where his low-flying plane came under intense and accurate fire from the Polish troops below. Miraculously, he was untouched, but the aircraft was riddled and the fuel tank so badly holed that the engine went dead as he approached to set down near his post. Making a dead-stick, or unpowered, landing, he quickly ordered up more strikes on the Polish ground defenses.

Elsewhere on the southern part of the Polish frontier, other Stuka units were flying ground-support missions. Near the Polish town of Wielun, 12 miles from the border, a wing of 30 Stukas led by Major Oskar Dinort went after Polish troops that were trying to reinforce the

Adolf Hitler strides from the cabin of a Ju 52 transport for a firsthand view of the fighting in Poland. The Führer left the conduct of the campaign mainly in the hands of his generals but made almost daily visits to the front, often by plane.

battlefront. As he approached Wielun, Dinort saw an enemy column snaking along the main road—cavalry from the look of it. Signaling his Stukas to follow, he banked left and dove straight for the Polish column.

As his plane plunged earthward, the whine of its propeller was joined by a high-pitched scream as the sirens attached to the Stuka's fixed landing gear began spinning; most Stukas were equipped with these sirens, called trumpets of Jericho, which added an extra element of terror to their attacks. Then Dinort extended the slatlike air brakes under the wings to slow his headlong dive, and the screech of the air passing through the brakes compounded the unearthly din. At about 3,000 feet, he released the 550-pound bomb carried under the plane's belly. To drop bombs at a lower altitude was perilous, since a Stuka could not be pulled out of its 350-mile-per-hour dive abruptly—the stress would have been too great on both men and machine—and it lost an additional 1,500 feet of altitude before leveling off and climbing back upward.

In theory, dive bombing was simple: An aircraft aimed vertically at a target before releasing its bombs should score a bull's-eye every time, the lateral speed of the plane being zero in relation to the target. In practice, Stuka pilots seldom achieved vertical dives, but they often screamed downward at 80 degrees, and that proved accurate enough. A man needed "dive nerve"—in pilots' jargon—to hurtle toward the ground in this fashion, watching the landscape below grow larger with frightening rapidity. He was fortified by the knowledge that the Stuka had great structural solidity. This strength came at a price, however. It made the Stuka heavy and therefore relatively slow: Top speed in level flight was about 235 miles per hour in the thin air at 15,000 feet.

For troops under attack, both the unholy noise of the diving Stuka and the awareness that a bomb would soon be whistling at them was a still greater test of nerve. Even if a man stood his ground and fired back in hopes of hitting the pilot, it seemed likely that the Stuka would come straight down and annihilate him anyway. Most soldiers fled when this nightmare weapon plummeted toward them.

Major Dinort, after releasing his main bomb, went into a tight climbing turn to evade the light antiaircraft fire snaking up toward his plane and looked back at the road near Wielun. A geyser of earth and black smoke erupted just beside the thoroughfare, and he saw the Polish riders and their horses scattering in every direction. He watched as the other Stukas repeated the process, smashing the road and the two-mile-long column of Polish troops still trying to make their way toward the front. After this attack, Dinort's planes re-formed to hit elsewhere, this time with the 110-pound bombs carried under their wings. Their target was a large farmhouse that appeared to be serving as a Polish headquarters. It disappeared under a pall of writhing smoke.

Later in the afternoon of September 1 the same Polish troop concentration was found by other planes on the prowl. In all, 90 dive bombers and level bombers blasted the 3,000-man cavalry brigade, destroying it as a fighting force.

The next day Dinort's unit was back in action again, making a remarkably precise attack, along with another Stuka squadron, on the railroad station at Piotrkow. They caught a Polish infantry division detraining from the railroad cars that had brought them forward. The division was smashed and never reached the front. Not one Polish fighter had appeared to oppose these attacks. Not one Stuka had been shot down.

The only Luftwaffe planes to meet serious resistance from the Polish Air Force on the first day of the War were 90 He 111s that took off from Hanover in northern Germany in the afternoon—when the fog and cloud had dispersed—to head for Warsaw, the center of Polish aircraft production as well as the nation's capital and communications hub. Their target was the large Okecie airfield southwest of the city and the nearby state-owned PZL airframe works.

As the German bombers neared the field, they were met by a swarm of some 30 P.11 fighters. The Poles, pressing their attacks to point-

A three-plane formation of Stukas descends on a target in Poland. With their banshee-like sirens, acrobatic dives and terrifying accuracy, the Stukas were held up as a symbol of unstoppable German might by the Reich's propagandists.

blank range, so unnerved the German air crews that the Heinkel pilots broke formation and jettisoned their bombs helter-skelter over the countryside. The escorting German Me 110s jumped into the fray, trying to drive the fighters away from the wheeling bombers. A melee of roaring, diving, twisting planes ensued as the battle spread over some 20 square miles of sky. Within a few minutes, the Poles had lost five fighters, shot down by withering bursts from the heavy armament carried by the Me 110s—two forward-firing 20-millimeter cannon and four machine guns. It was the first air-to-air combat of World War II.

A second air battle developed two days later, on September 3, when another German raid on Warsaw also prodded into life a wasps' nest of P.11 fighters, which angrily buzzed upward to disperse the

German formations. This time, the maneuverable Polish fighters managed to shoot down three of the faster but clumsier twin-engined Messerschmitts. Two P.11s were downed by Me 110s. However, no Polish fighter seemed to have fallen to the guns of the Heinkel bombers, a fact that disturbed the more prescient German air commanders, who concluded that their Heinkel and Dornier bombers lacked adequate defensive armament. Each had only a single gunner working a hand-held light machine gun to beat off attacks from the rear. This shortcoming was to prove a greater problem when the Luftwaffe met more formidable opponents in years to come.

The failure of Polish fighters to intercept the raiders in significant numbers except over Warsaw was not due to a lack of planes: General Kesselring, the chief of Luftflotte 1, estimated that the initial attacks on airfields had destroyed only 30 Polish aircraft before they could take off. Most of Poland's combat planes had been dispersed to small, well-camouflaged fields. However, these auxiliary airstrips lacked adequate telephone and teletype hookups and had no early-warning systems. As a result, the Polish aircraft, although safe from German bombs, could not be mobilized into a coherent defensive screen.

"We were at an airfield 20 miles from Poznan," recalled Major Mieczyslaw Mumler, a Polish squadron leader. "I immediately recognized that without advance warning, without knowing what was coming, it is not so easy to intercept, and with so many messages coming in from headquarters in Warsaw, communications broke down." Isolated in this manner, squadrons such as Mumler's generally stayed on the ground on September 1; thereafter, they made scattered attacks on German formations but, greatly outnumbered, could do little to repel the invaders.

The spirited defense of Warsaw was possible because the city had just put in an early-warning system. According to Polish Air Force Major F. Kalinowski, "a net of observation posts to provide early warning of approaching enemy aircraft had been established around Warsaw in the summer of 1939, and these posts were to pass information by radio and telephone to the Pursuit Brigade's operations room, from which all 'scramble' orders were given." With this advance notice, the Warsaw squadrons could get into the air in time to meet the oncoming Heinkels and Me 110s.

But even around Warsaw the Poles fought a doomed battle. A member of the Warsaw Pursuit Brigade, Lieutenant Aleksander Gabszewicz, later said, "We realized that the Germans had many more superior aircraft than we did. We still tried to engage them in battles, and we did. Mostly we had success against Heinkels and Stukas because they went as slow as, or even slower than, our planes, but when it came to Dorniers we had only a few successes when we caught them unprepared."

Yet another handicap for the Poles was a lack of spare parts with which to repair planes that suffered damage during combat. The German raiders had obliterated most of the Polish Air Force's repair shops and other ground facilities. Even lightly damaged P.11 fighters were write-offs, grounded and out of action.

For a week, the Warsaw squadrons continued to put up an energetic fight in spite of all their disadvantages, and on September 6 they had their best day, bringing down 15 German aircraft. "But on September 7," Major Kalinowski remembered, "the brigade was forced to withdraw to the southeast of Warsaw, as the airfields north of the capital were under constant air attack."

Except in the Warsaw area, resistance by the Polish Air Force had become insignificant by Sunday, September 3. The Luftwaffe could therefore concentrate additional forces on the destruction of the Polish Army and the disruption of the enemy rail system. Even the single-engined Me 109 fighters turned to strafing, recalled Captain Hannes Gentzen, the leader of a fighter squadron based in Upper Silesia. "Shooting up locomotives developed into a particular specialty with us. For this we would be in *Ketten*"—formations of three planes—"down to two or three meters above the ground. While one would shoot at the locomotive, the other two would rake the train with their machine guns in order to prevent anyone getting off and making use of his weapons."

The planes of Luftflotten 1 and 4 continued to range ahead of the German tanks throughout the first 10 days of the campaign, cutting up and disorganizing the Polish forces that stood in the way of the lightning advance. "In the air, powerful formations of German aircraft, but not one Polish, passed constantly overhead," remembered Lieutenant General Wladyslaw Anders, who commanded cavalry and armored detachments that attempted to blunt the drive of Bock's Third Army, thrusting southward out of East Prussia. With only light armored cars and mounted riflemen to face the German tanks—a few of them 20-ton Panzer Mark IV models armed with 75-millimeter guns—Anders decided to retreat behind the natural barrier of the Vistula River and there set up a defensive line. He soon found that orderly withdrawal was nearly impossible; the roads were choked with civilian refugees and the remnants of a demoralized infantry regiment that was fleeing from Bock's tanks and Kesselring's planes. "Hundreds of German aircraft," Anders recalled, "bombed the retiring columns, and even made attacks on soldiers moving in small groups across country."

When Anders' force, after a prolonged retreat, finally joined some other Polish units south of Warsaw, their combined attempt to form a coherent front and deliver a counterattack was frustrated by the ever-present Luftwaffe. German bombers hammered the Polish concentration, and observation planes discovered that the Poles' right flank was unprotected. In short order, German units circled the open flank and surrounded the Polish force. Anders and some of his remaining men managed to flee the trap, dodging through forests at night toward eastern Poland, but his force was finished as a fighting unit.

In the south the story was much the same. Richthofen's Henschels and Stukas and the other planes of Luftflotte 4, sometimes flying eight

or more missions a day, so thoroughly paralyzed the Polish defensive positions around the towns of Dzialoszyn and Czestochowa that Reichenau's Tenth Army panzers sped straight through them in their race for Warsaw. As the panzers churned on into Poland, the entire Polish 7th Division was trapped by a swift envelopment near Czestochowa. After a single day of relentless strafing and bombing by Luftflotte 4, the division surrendered en masse. For the first time in history an air force had caused a ground unit of division size to lay down its arms.

The planes of Luftflotte 4 repeated this performance five days later when an even larger Polish force was trapped by fast-moving panzers south of the city of Radom. In the sort of fight later called a caldron battle—the enemy troops ringed as if in a large cooking pot—the Luftwaffe visited utter devastation on the Poles. One squadron leader recalled that, during the battle, Stukas located the enemy by following the attacking German tanks, which had large white crosses painted on their backs for easier air recognition: "Wherever they went, we came across throngs of Polish troops, against which our 100-pound fragmentation bombs were deadly. After that we went almost down to the deck firing our machine guns. The confusion was indescribable."

The Luftwaffe climaxed its ground-support operations by helping to thwart the one potentially dangerous counterattack the Poles managed to mount. An entire Polish army group of four infantry divisions and two cavalry brigades, originally deployed close to the German-Polish frontier near Poznan, had fallen back to a position near Kutno and the Bzura River some 65 miles due west of Warsaw. Bypassed by the German pincers slicing toward Warsaw to the south and north, the 170,000-man Army of Poznan, commanded by General Tadeusz Kutrzeba, had remained intact. On the morning of September 9, its best troops swarmed across the Bzura and attacked the lightly protected northern flank of General von Rundstedt's Army Group South, sending the nearest German division, the 30th Infantry, reeling backward. Had the Poles been able to press on, they could have cut off Reichenau's fast-moving Tenth Army both from its supplies and from General Jacob Blaskowitz' Eighth Army, a slower-advancing formation made up largely of infantry, which was assigned to protect Reichenau's flank and rear.

The Luftwaffe, alerted by Rundstedt to this impending catastrophe, quickly sent Richthofen's air division to bomb the counterattacking Poles. While the Eighth Army marched to the rescue of the 30th Division, squadrons of Richthofen's Stukas dive-bombed the Polish advance guard, and his 30 remaining Henschel 123 attack planes made low-level bombing and strafing runs, showering the Poles with antipersonnel fragmentation bombs and flambos. The Polish troops, never before under air attack, scattered in confusion, and their horses—both draft animals and cavalry mounts—went mad with panic.

These air assaults were followed by higher level-bombing runs by squadrons of Heinkel and Dornier bombers. Then came waves of Me 110s that flew back and forth over the Polish formations, strafing

In the wake of a deadly visit by German bombers, smoke billows from the Warsaw gasworks. After the Luftwaffe had interrupted vital city services, it rained incendiary bombs on the homes of the defiant citizens, who had turned the Polish capital into an armed citadel.

any vehicles, horses or men that had survived the previous attacks. On the night of September 12, what was left of the Polish advance force retreated across the Bzura under the cover of darkness.

The German Eighth Army now moved to encircle the Army of Poznan, joined in this task by General Günther von Kluge's Fourth Army coming down from the north and elements of Reichenau's Tenth, which temporarily wheeled about to drive westward. The Luftwaffe returned to the assault, hitting the Poles from every direction. For several more days, the Army of Poznan continued to resist and to try to break out of its ever-shrinking pocket. Finally, on September 17, its battered units began to surrender. All resistance ended on the 19th. The German bag of Polish prisoners totaled some 155,000 men. Summing up the Luftwaffe's attacks on his forces, General Kutrzeba later said that "every movement, every troop concentration, every line of advance came under pulverizing bombardment from the air. It was just hell on earth."

Although some Luftwaffe airmen reveled in the bloodshed, others expressed unease. Major Walter Grabmann, whose wing of Me 110s was ordered to fire on anything that moved in an area along the Vistula, wistfully summed up his air crews' feelings after a debriefing at their East Prussian base: "Oh, for a fair and decent dogfight!"

Ten days before the Army of Poznan ceased to exist, advance elements of the Tenth Army's panzers had reached the outskirts of Warsaw. There the Germans ran into powerful resistance. Polish artillery within the city directed such savage fire on the 35th Panzer and 12th Rifle Regiments as they advanced through the suburbs that the German units were forced to retire. Casualties were heavy.

Ironically, the Poles' effective use of artillery inside Warsaw hastened the city's fall. Up until now, the Luftwaffe had abided by the restrictions of Article 25 of the 1907 Hague Convention on the conduct of war, which forbids attacks on undefended cities. The first waves of German bombers dropped only surrender-or-else leaflets on the Polish capital. But as the city's defenders, some 100,000 soldiers in all, continued to defy and harass the attackers from foxholes, street barricades and fortified buildings, the German air arm—having given what it considered fair warning—began a final, stunning assault.

Richthofen, who was assigned the job of forcing Warsaw's stubborn defenders to surrender, assembled some 400 aircraft. To his intense fury, the He 111s he needed to carry the phosphorus incendiary bombs earmarked for the operation were withdrawn, beginning September 12, and sent by a nervous Göring to western Germany to guard against any possible Allied moves against the Reich's other frontier. Richthofen found a solution, however, pressing into service 30 lumbering trimotor Ju 52 transport planes temporarily attached to his force. Loading them with the two-pound incendiaries, he placed two soldiers aboard each plane to shovel the bombs out of the side cargo doors, and the Ju 52s joined the formations of dive bombers in shuttling over Poland's capital when the main assault began at 8 a.m. on September 25.

Performing before an audience of Wehrmacht troops, a Heinkel 111 sweeps in to stoke the fires already raging throughout Warsaw. With the Polish Air Force obliterated, the Luftwaffe was challenged only by scattered antiaircraft fire as it pounded the city into submission.

By midday Warsaw was aflame. A huge column of smoke rose to a height of 10,000 feet and spread across the sky, and by afternoon the pilots reported difficulty identifying targets through the dense smoke clouds. After dark this canopy took on a red tinge. It was reflecting the glowing embers of a once-handsome metropolis, pulverized by 500 tons of explosives and carbonized by 72 tons of incendiaries. On September 27, after the city had endured 1,776 bombing sorties in the space of two days, the Warsaw commander asked for a cessation of hostilities. On the 30th the garrison marched out of the city and piled its arms. With the fall of Warsaw nearly all Polish resistance ended.

The speed of the German conquest of Poland astounded the world. A new form of warfare had been unveiled, one in which the airplane played a vital, indeed crucial, role. The German Army had outnumbered the Polish ground forces by a considerable margin—1,500,000 men against the million that the Poles had managed to put into the field. But it was not weight of numbers that had enabled the panzers to reach Warsaw's outskirts in little more than a week or to crush the Polish Army in less than a month. The key to the German success, in the words of British military historian J. F. C. Fuller, was "the velocity of aircraft and armored forces operating as one integrated force."

Germany's efficiency in war astonished the Soviet Union as much as it did other nations, but Stalin was not at all surprised by the target or the timing. In late August he and Hitler had signed a secret agreement to divide up their hapless neighbor. On September 17, Stalin ordered his troops to flood across the undefended Soviet-Polish border, and by the end of the month they had gobbled up the eastern part of the country.

The cost of the campaign to the Luftwaffe was light, considering the demands made upon its planes and men. In all, 285 aircraft were lost, most to antiaircraft fire and some to the inevitable accidents, such as poor landings by tired pilots, that are a part of all operational flying. Of various aircraft types involved in the lightning war, the Ju 87 Stuka dive bomber had enjoyed the greatest success—in good part because it met almost no opposition. Hitler's propagandists made the most of its destructive performance and devastating effect on morale, hoping to serve Germany's strategic interests by paralyzing everyone else's will to fight.

As for the Polish Air Force, a number of its pilots survived the disaster to fight again. On September 17, when the outcome of the invasion was beyond doubt, they were ordered by their commander, General Pilot Wladyslaw Jan Kalkus, to make their way southeastward toward neutral Rumania. They commandeered whatever flyable planes they could find, hitched rides in southbound automobiles or trekked to the Rumanian border on foot. From there they generally headed for Italy or Greece, both still neutral, and thence to France and finally to England, where they were welcomed into the hard-pressed RAF. During the Battle of Britain they proved courageous to the point of recklessness in their anger at the Germans.

Major Mumler was among the last of those to flee. Before leaving his country, he flew his P.11 all over Poland to stay out of the hands of the fast-advancing Germans and then the invading Russians. Once, when his plane was low on fuel, he landed on a road near a Polish column that fortuitously had a spare barrel of gasoline left among its supplies. On his last landing in Poland he put down on a rough field and damaged his tail wheel. His plane could make only one more flight, he knew, because the next landing was certain to cause irreparable damage to its entire tail assembly. "I say to myself," Mumler later wrote, "it is my last takeoff. I talk to my plane—she had a human soul—saying, 'you must serve me, my friend.' I cross myself and take off for Rumania, where we went for holidays before the War, so I knew it quite well. It is almost dark but I must go on and I cross the River Dniester on the border of Poland and Rumania, then the River Prut, and I head downriver for the airfield at Czerniowce. At last I see underneath me an airdrome full of aircraft. I suddenly remember that I had forgotten to check my fuel. I look and it's on zero! I land and the second before I touch down my propeller stops."

From Rumania, Mumler traveled by train to Belgrade and then Athens, and from there by ship to Marseilles. After the fall of France, he flew a French plane to Algeria and took a train, which was packed with other Polish refugees, to Casablanca. At last a British convoy arrived and carried the Poles to Liverpool. "On September 17, one year exactly after my escape from Poland, I joined the Battle of Britain in the great Polish 302 Squadron."

As for the victorious German airmen and their commanders, many believed Hitler's professions that, after Poland, he had no further conquests in view. In truth, however, the dazzling success of this blitzkrieg had merely whetted the Führer's appetite for others. Immediately after Warsaw's fall, he ordered his High Command to complete plans for an assault on the nations to the west, and within months the skills of the Luftwaffe would be in greater demand than ever. 〜〜

Field Marshal Hermann Göring congratulates German airmen on their victory in Poland. The stunning swiftness of the Luftwaffe triumph gave credence to Göring's boast that his air corps stood "ready to carry out every command of the Führer with lightning speed and undreamed-of might."

Small bombers for quick strikes

Goaded by dreams of conquest, German military planners focused on the development of short- to medium-range bombers that could support Wehrmacht units on the ground or attack ships at sea.

The Junkers 87 dive bomber seldom flew farther than 400 miles, yet it could consistently deliver its explosives within 40 yards of the mark. Likewise, the Heinkel 111 and Junkers 88 had a limited range of 1,200 miles but were particularly effective when used to cripple an enemy's supply lines by cutting roads and railways. Even

the hefty Dornier 217 and the jet-powered Arado 234, which was designed for high-altitude reconnaissance missions, were equipped for diving attacks so they could pinpoint military targets. Only the Heinkel 115 failed in its intended role as a torpedo plane when its slow speed proved to be a hazard on runs.

The bombers shown here and on the following pages are all improved late models; the parenthetical dates are the years the aircraft became operational. Planes on facing pages are presented in scale.

HEINKEL HE 111 P-1 (1939)
The He 111, derived from an outmoded single-engined precursor, had a glass nose with a top panel that could be opened to give the pilot an outside view during landings in poor weather.

JUNKERS JU 87 G-1 (1943)
Better known as the Stuka, the Ju 87 forged a reputation as the ultimate dive bomber in the early months of the War. Some later models, like this plane that belonged to famed pilot Hans-Ulrich Rudel, were rigged with twin 37-mm. antiaircraft guns and put to work smashing tanks.

HEINKEL HE 115 B-2 (1940)
Conceived as a torpedo bomber, the slender-bodied, 200-mph Heinkel floatplane found its niche laying mines and escorting convoys. The pontoons on this plane are reinforced with steel skids for landing on snow during the occupation of Norway.

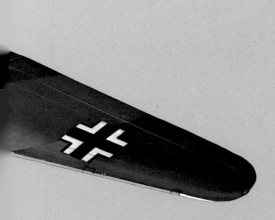

JUNKERS JU 88 A-4 (1943)
The Ju 88 was the Luftwaffe's jack-of-all-trades. A potent bomber that could travel at 290 mph, it also served as fighter, torpedo plane, missile launcher and tank buster. Nearly 15,000 were produced—far more than any other German bomber.

DORNIER DO 217 E-5 (1943)
The Luftwaffe's heaviest bomber when introduced, the Do 217 was designed to range 1,300 miles with an 8,800-pound payload of bombs. This plane is armed with two radio-controlled missiles, which were used to attack Allied shipping. The missiles were guided by the plane's bombardier.

ARADO AR 234 B-2 (1944)
Nicknamed the Blitz by the Germans, the single-seat Arado jet was faster, at 460 mph, than any Allied interceptor and could carry three 1,100-pound bombs. Only 210 were built before the War's end.

2

Two victorious aerial assaults

At 6:15 on the morning of April 9, 1940, nine transport planes with black German crosses on their wings flew over a Danish coastal fort on the island of Masnedö. Small figures began tumbling from the planes; in seconds more than 100 parachutes blossomed against the silvery dawn sky. Ninety-six German paratroops, dressed in baggy, smocklike gray green jackets and bowl-shaped steel helmets, floated to earth, along with a number of large metal canisters containing extra weapons and ammunition. History's first combat operation involving parachuted troops was under way.

Some of these invaders from the sky quickly shucked their parachute harnesses and rushed the fort's dumfounded sentries, who found German machine pistols aimed at their heads before they fully comprehended that they were now at war. The remainder of the fort's garrison, caught in sleepy-eyed confusion by the attack, also surrendered without a fight.

Another detachment of the paratroops, moving with equal swiftness, set up machine guns covering a long, vital road-and-rail bridge that linked Masnedö with Seeland, the island on which the Danish capital of Copenhagen is located. From the bridge the railroad stretched north to Copenhagen and south to a rail-ferry port just across a short stretch of sea from Germany. The Danish guards on the bridge, outnumbered and outgunned, surrendered. In one bloodless stroke the Germans had captured one of the most important bridge links of the seagirt kingdom.

The operation was a triumph, and the triumph was the Luftwaffe's. Germany's paratroops, unlike the airborne forces that were being developed by other nations, were part of the air force rather than the Army—an arrangement wrought by fiat of Luftwaffe chief Hermann Göring, who had once proclaimed that "everything that flies belongs to me." (He extended his authority even wider than that; Germany's antiaircraft gunners also wore Luftwaffe uniforms.)

In a second airborne operation that same morning, a platoon of Luftwaffe paratroops captured two strategic airfields near Aalborg on Denmark's Jutland peninsula. Again the invading Germans met virtually no resistance. Nor was there much resistance that morning in the capital of Copenhagen itself. Shortly after dawn a battalion of 1,000 German infantry, smuggled into Copenhagen harbor by night aboard the troopship *Hansestadt Danzig,* stepped briskly ashore near the statue

Cruising under dense cloud cover to avoid high-flying Allied fighters, Heinkel 111 bombers lead the German thrust into France in May 1940. In the first 12 hours of Hitler's campaign in the West, Luftwaffe bombers attacked 72 Allied air bases in Holland, Belgium and France.

In late spring of 1940, a German paratrooper—one of nearly 1,000 who jumped in this operation—descends near Narvik, Norway, to aid battle-weary ground troops trying to recapture the strategic port. The Allies evacuated Narvik on June 8, just as the Germans were gearing up for an all-out assault.

of Hans Christian Andersen's Little Mermaid and marched smartly through the city toward Amalienborg Palace, residence of Denmark's 70-year-old King Christian X.

As the German battalion neared the palace, a detachment of sentries belonging to the King's Guard, resplendent in blue uniforms and bearskin shakos, cocked their rifles and opened fire. The Germans took cover and fired back, killing six guardsmen and wounding a dozen. But before this unequal battle was minutes old, several formations of Heinkel 111 and Dornier 17 bombers roared over the city. They dropped no bombs, but the clear implication that the Luftwaffe could easily turn beautiful Copenhagen into another Warsaw convinced the King that any resistance to the Germans would be futile. He ordered an immediate cease-fire; by 8:34, about two and a half hours after the first paratroops jumped from their Junkers 52 transports, Hitler had added 16,000 square miles of territory to his fast-growing empire.

The quick seizure of Denmark was but part of Hitler's stunningly successful campaign in April of 1940 to secure his northern flank before pursuing his greater design: the conquest of the Low Countries and France. The two campaigns—in Scandinavia and a month later across the plains of western Europe—were among the most brilliant military operations of modern times. Like the four-week blitzkrieg in Poland, they were made possible largely by the power of the Luftwaffe's planes and the expertise of the men who flew them. Success also hinged on the effectiveness of the Luftwaffe's new weapon: airborne shock troops that were dropped in the enemy's territory to capture, as in Denmark, key bridges and airfields.

The Luftwaffe added still another function to its repertoire during these campaigns—riding to the rescue, much like the cavalry of old, when some part of the German generals' complex schemes misfired or the enemy mounted an unexpected threat to the entire enterprise. The men of the Luftwaffe taught the world a lesson in the extraordinary flexibility, as well as the crushing power, of the air weapon.

As the year 1940 began, Hitler had reason to fear that Germany's northern approaches were in peril. Berlin had picked up rumors that the British were hatching some sort of Scandinavian scheme, probably an invasion of Norway and a march from there into northern Sweden. The Führer was vividly aware that a British invasion of Norway could have crippling consequences for Germany. Besides placing the Royal Navy and Air Force on Germany's northern doorstep, such a move could sever the Reich's industrial life line: A majority of the iron ore that fed Hitler's war machine—11 million tons out of a total of 15 million in the first year of the War—came from the mining complex of Gällivare in the far north of Sweden. If British troops seized the Norwegian port of Narvik, only 133 miles overland from Gällivare, they could easily throttle the supply at its source.

To forestall the British—who were in fact planning a Scandinavian expedition—Hitler resolved to invade Norway himself. An added lure was Norway's long, fjord-notched coastline, which would give the German Navy's submarines and surface raiders cozy lairs from which to harry British shipping. Norway's airfields would serve the same function for the Luftwaffe. The Führer added tiny Denmark to his plan of conquest to provide a convenient steppingstone between Germany and Norway and an additional site for bomber bases facing the North Sea. Sweden, less exposed to any British armed adventures and willing to sell its raw materials to the Reich, would be allowed to remain neutral.

The planners of the campaign were forced by geography to invent a new, modified form of blitzkrieg. Low-lying Denmark with its many islands was not an ideal place to employ divisions of heavy tanks. Nor was Norway: Separated from Germany by the waters of the Kattegat and the Skagerrak, it was a land of precipitous and often snow-clad mountains. Clearly the invasion forces would have to be carried in by sea and air. And speed was mandatory, to surprise the Norwegian and Danish defenders and to have the larger ports and airfields firmly in German hands before British ships and planes could intervene. That was where the paratroops came in.

The Luftwaffe's paratroops had been organized—and were still commanded—by Lieutenant General Kurt Student, a dedicated professional soldier who had been a pilot in World War I. Student had assembled some of Germany's toughest young infantrymen and molded them into a *corps d'élite,* expert not only at jumping from planes but also at handling automatic weapons and demolition charges. Student's men became as dedicated as their leader. If a trooper panicked and refused to make a training jump, he was not punished; he

As commander of airborne troops during Germany's thrusts to the west, General Kurt Student displayed a boldness and efficiency that earned him the Knight's Cross of the Iron Cross. He was struck in the head by a sniper's bullet in Rotterdam on May 14, 1940, but recovered fully and returned to duty four months later.

was simply transferred to another unit. That was punishment enough.

By 1939 Student had his 7th Airborne Division ready for action. His troops were trained to go into combat either by parachuting from Ju 52 transport planes or by descending silently in large troop-carrying gliders that were towed to the target area by the same "Iron Annies," as the sturdy, corrugated, three-engined Junkers transports were nicknamed.

About eight platoons—totaling perhaps 325 paratroopers—from Student's 7th Airborne were assigned to the invasion of Norway, which began simultaneously with the Danish takeover, shortly after dawn on April 9. The task of these units was to capture a pair of vitally important airfields, one near the city of Stavanger on Norway's southwestern coast, and another near the capital of Oslo. After parachuting down, the aerial storm troopers were to wipe out the Norwegian machine-gun nests defending both airports. More Iron Annies could then be landed to disgorge larger detachments of infantry. When the airfields were under German control, Luftwaffe bombers and fighters would fly in, ready to beat off any raids mounted by British planes or to strike at any Royal Navy ships that ventured close to the Norwegian coast.

The drop on the airfield near Stavanger was another triumph of surprise and coordination—and a display of Luftwaffe daring as well. Captain Gunther Capito, leader of the flight of 12 Iron Annies headed for Stavanger, found the weather over the Skagerrak atrocious—cloud and pea-soup fog. "The whole squadron was swallowed up," Capito later reported. "Despite the closest formation, the nearest plane was like a phantom." Collision of two Ju 52s in the murk would be fatal to the crews and the dozen or so paratroopers inside each plane. And Capito knew that the planned approach to Stavanger led over rugged Norwegian mountains. If the cloud cover persisted, such an approach would be impossibly dangerous.

Capito nevertheless determined to press on. His courage was rewarded 60 miles from the Norwegian coast, where the clouds thinned and 11 of his Iron Annies emerged into the sunlight (one had become lost and landed in Denmark). Descending from 3,000 feet to 30 to avoid detection, the planes skimmed across the Norwegian coast, droned up a valley and then leaped over a string of sharp-ridged hills. Suddenly the airfield appeared before them. The paratroops dropped from the cargo doors at 400 feet, a perilously low altitude, but one that left the troopers hanging defenseless below their silk canopies for only about 20 seconds. Capito's Ju 52s then scooted for home.

As Lieutenant Freiherr von Brandis' paratroopers hit the airstrip, they were caught in a hail of machine-gun fire. Instantly, two Messerschmitt 110s roared down to strafe the Norwegian defenders with their 20-millimeter cannon, and the paratroops were soon able to rush the Norwegian gun emplacements. Within half an hour, well before the Norwegian Army garrison in Stavanger could react, the airfield was in German hands. Much of the rest of the German invasion of Norway went almost as swiftly. Naval task forces carrying occupation troops arrived off six of Norway's main ports almost simultaneously on the morning of April 9. In some places Norwegian troops resisted, but by noon the bewildered citizens of the ports were watching German troops marching through their streets.

The capture of Oslo, the most important part of the operation, was another matter, however, and only some implausible heroics by a handful of Luftwaffe pilots rescued that part of the German scheme.

The trouble began just before dawn as the naval task force assigned to Oslo, led by the brand-new 12,000-ton cruiser *Blücher,* steamed through a narrow section of the fjord leading to the Norwegian capital. At this spot, 18 miles south of the city, stood an ancient fort named Oscarsborg, armed with three 11-inch guns (ironically, made in Germany in 1905). The garrison opened fire at the mist-shrouded intruders, and two 760-pound projectiles slammed into the *Blücher.* As the cruiser's ammunition caught fire, racking the ship with explosions, two shore-launched torpedoes hit her below the water line. Within minutes the *Blücher* turned turtle and went to the bottom, carrying with her more than 1,000 crewmen and troops who were to have helped occupy Oslo. The rest of the task force backed off, not daring to challenge Oscarsborg's guns; the remaining infantrymen were disembarked 30 miles south of their destination.

Now Oslo's capture depended entirely on the airborne troops being ferried from Germany aboard two waves of Ju 52 transports to seize the city's airfield. The men engaged in this operation were also in for some nasty surprises. The first wave of 29 Iron Annies, carrying more than 200 paratroopers, ran into the same fog over the Skagerrak that was plaguing Captain Capito and his force en route to Stavanger. Lieutenant Martin Drewes, commander of the Oslo-bound transports, was alarmed when a section leader astern reported by radio that two of his Ju 52s seemed to have vanished. In fact, as Drewes must have suspected, they had collided in the fog and crashed, killing all on board. This was too much for Drewes. He radioed the headquarters of *Fliegerkorps X,* the 10th Air Corps, in Hamburg, responsible for the Luftwaffe's part of the Scandinavian campaign, that he was turning back and heading for the recently captured Danish airfields at Aalborg.

Lieutenant General Hans Geisler, commander of Fliegerkorps X, was now in a painful dilemma. The second wave of Ju 52s was already in the air, flying 20 minutes behind Drewes's first wave. The airborne infantry in these transports were not equipped to make a parachute jump; the planes would have to land at Oslo's airfield to unload their troops—a suicidal proposition if paratroops had not first neutralized the field's defenses, since Norwegian machine guns would riddle any slow-landing transport. Geisler issued the only sensible order: The entire second wave must also turn back, immediately. It seemed that Oslo would not be captured until the infantry put ashore by the naval task force managed to march northward to the Norwegian capital.

Then events took another twist. The second wave of transports was under the command of a Luftwaffe airborne infantry officer, a Captain Wagner, who refused to believe Geisler's recall order when it came over his plane's radio. It sounded, Wagner thought, like an enemy trick rather than an authentic message. Besides, visibility improved as the planes passed over southern Norway. Wagner decided to continue to Oslo and land his troops.

While all of this was taking place, eight Me 110s had flown through the fog into clear weather south of Oslo. Their job was to strafe the airfield to prepare the way for the paratroops. They soon had troubles of their own. Hardly had the pilots emerged from the last layers of mist to see Oslo in the distance when seven of the minuscule Norwegian air force's British-made Gloster Gladiator fighters pounced upon them from out of the sun. The battle was short and sharp. Two Messerschmitts were shot down while Lieutenant Helmut Lent, who later became a top Luftwaffe fighter ace, downed a Gladiator.

The other Norwegian fighters soon withdrew, and the Me 110s began strafing Oslo's airfield, shooting up a pair of Gladiators on the runway and trying to eliminate the field's machine-gun defenses, as planned,

Given cover by a Luftwaffe gunner, gray-uniformed shock troops pile out of a Junkers 52 transport plane at Oslo-Fornebu airport during the German invasion of Norway in April 1940. A total of 30,000 troops were airlifted into the country.

before the paratroops arrived. But no transport planes appeared, and before long, red warning lights in the Messerschmitt cockpits began to blink on as fuel gauges sank toward empty.

At last some Ju 52s droned in overhead. No parachutes appeared, however; the planes were the infantry transports that had flown on despite the recall order. Lieutenant Hansen, the Messerschmitt leader, watched in horror as one of the Ju 52s began to descend for a landing. Norwegian ground fire tore into the Iron Annie, killing Captain Wagner and wounding several of the troops. The pilot of the riddled transport pushed his throttles forward and climbed back out of range.

Hansen realized that something had to be done quickly, before more transports tried to land—and before his own Messerschmitts littered the landscape for lack of fuel. The only possible course of action, he decided, was for the fighter crews to capture the field themselves. Hansen ordered Lent to try a landing while he and his other four remaining pilots continued to strafe the Norwegian machine-gun emplacements.

Lent had shut down his starboard engine to save fuel and did not have the control he needed to make a smooth touchdown. First it seemed he would crash before reaching the airport boundary. Applying power to his port engine, he made it to the runway, but he was then going too fast to stop on the short strip. His tires screeched on the tarmac as he jammed on the brakes. Then, as bullets from the Norwegian guns crisscrossed around Lent's Messerschmitt, an Iron Annie landed on an intersecting runway. A collision seemed inevitable, but Lent's plane careened through the intersection a split second before the Ju 52 got there. The Messerschmitt hurtled beyond the end of the runway and down a bank. Neither Lent nor his gunner was hurt. They climbed from the wreckage, carrying with them their plane's rear machine gun for use on the Norwegian defenders.

Hansen was next, his starboard engine blowing steaming coolant after being hit on his last pass over the airfield defenses. He neatly nursed his Me 110 down onto the runway and brought the plane to a halt. By the time the remaining four Me 110s were on the ground, the Norwegians had abandoned their guns, most of which had been fired so furiously that they had jammed from overheating. The circling Ju 52s then began to land, and the infantrymen they carried fanned out to capture the last Norwegian defenders. Finally the paratroops arrived, flying in from Denmark. There was no longer any need for them to jump, so their transports landed and the troopers stepped from them like so many tourists. The airfield, captured by half a dozen Luftwaffe pilots and their gunners, was safely under German control.

The next act of the implausible drama was directed by Captain Eberhard Spiller, the air attaché at the German embassy in Oslo, who had driven to the airfield before dawn to greet the arriving force. Taking command, he formed the German troops—some seven companies in all—into a line of march that included a small brass band that had come in on one of the last transports. Before the local Norwegian Army garrison could mobilize, Spiller had brazenly paraded this force through the streets of downtown Oslo, taking possession of the city, the first metropolis ever to fall to troops that had descended from the sky.

The capture of the capital had taken time, however, and the delay gave Norway's King Haakon VII, his family and a number of government leaders the chance to flee. Moving from one Norwegian town to another and staying well ahead of the enemy, the King refused repeated German demands for Norway's surrender and ordered his country's small army to resist the invaders. Most of the Norwegian Army units were swiftly subdued by the Germans, but some fought on, buttressed by an Allied expeditionary force that arrived belatedly to contest the German invasion. Hitler, who had hoped to take control of Norway as speedily and peacefully as he had Denmark, with a captured and compliant monarch smoothing the way, instead found his forces embroiled in a frustrating struggle. Two months would pass before the Germans could claim total victory in Norway. The fight might have lasted longer—or might never have been won by Germany at all—if the Luftwaffe had not proved to be capable of inspired and bold improvisation when the occasion demanded it.

The most crucial demonstration of this ability came when some 25,000 Allied troops seemed about to wrest the port of Narvik, key to the Reich's all-important Swedish iron ore supply, from a small German force holding the town. Major General Eduard Dietl and his 2,000 men from the Wehrmacht's 3rd Mountain Division had been ashore at Narvik only one day when a flotilla of British destroyers rammed its way into the harbor on April 10 and sank or badly damaged every German ship in sight, including those that had delivered the occupation force from Germany. During their withdrawal down Narvik's fjord, the British also blew up the merchantman carrying Dietl's ammunition reserve. Three days later the Royal Navy attacked again—this time bringing the big guns of the battleship *Warspite* to bear—and destroyed virtually every remaining German ship afloat at Narvik and in the neighboring fjords.

On April 16 the large Allied force of Britons, Frenchmen and Poles landed at Harstad, 30 miles to the north, and began advancing toward Narvik in company with Norwegian troops. Dietl and his men were in desperate straits, cut off in their remote Arctic post without naval support and with no German ground troop reinforcements within hundreds of miles. Dietl's only hope of avoiding surrender was the Luftwaffe.

The Luftwaffe immediately sent a dozen Ju 52s loaded with mountain artillery pieces, ammunition and gunners. For want of an airfield, the aircraft landed on a frozen lake 10 miles from Narvik—an unnerving experience for the first pilot to touch down, not knowing whether the ice would withstand the impact of a plane that weighed, with its full load, 12 tons. The ice held. Dietl now at least had some artillery to help his outnumbered force repel the first probing Allied attacks.

The Luftwaffe soon stepped up its airlift operation under the able and innovative Lieutenant General Hans-Jürgen Stumpff, who on

A British trawler (top) and merchant vessels become easy marks for a Luftwaffe bomber prowling the North Sea in 1940. These targets—all of which were sunk during a single mission—were photographed by a cameraman crouched in the glass-enclosed nose of a Heinkel 111K.

May 1 became the commander of the newly formed Luftflotte 5, with responsibility for Scandinavia. Stumpff sent relays of Ju 52s winging toward Narvik with tons of rations and ammunition. Small detachments of paratroops jumped into the snowy wilderness to provide reinforcements. Stumpff also persuaded Luftwaffe headquarters in Berlin to send him a squadron of Junkers 88s, the most advanced German bombers, which had gone into production only a few months before. This sleek aircraft, powered by twin radial engines, could attain a top speed of about 300 miles per hour and, of more importance to Stumpff at the moment, could cruise 750 miles on a distant mission and still return to base. He also obtained some Ju 87Rs, new Stukas with extra fuel tanks.

With these reinforcements, Stumpff undertook to bomb every Royal Navy ship that ventured anywhere near Narvik, and he systematically destroyed the port facilities at Harstad, where supplies for the Allied force advancing on Narvik were landed and stored. The British cruiser *Curlew* was sunk, along with a destroyer and a troopship, and the battleship *Resolution* and two more cruisers were badly damaged and had to limp home to Britain. In these actions, the Luftwaffe demonstrated that the bomber was the master of even the most heavily armored warship, especially when the ship had no fighter cover from land- or carrier-based aircraft. It was a lesson the Japanese learned well and put to dramatic use 18 months later at Pearl Harbor.

The Luftwaffe's work, combined with poor weather and lack of Arctic equipment, slowed the Allied advance to a crawl, saving General Dietl's paltry force. The Allies took more than six weeks to cover the 30 miles from Harstad to Narvik. When they captured the port at last on May 28, Dietl and his troops had escaped to safety in the nearby mountains.

Although they had reached their goal, the Allies knew that Luftwaffe bombers would make holding and resupplying the town difficult. A handful of RAF fighters were rushed to landing strips hastily cleared of snow near Narvik, but they could not wrest control of the air from the Luftwaffe, and the British, by then battling the Germans in the Low Countries and France, could not afford to send more planes to Norway. It was clear that the British could not hold on.

Prime Minister Winston Churchill gave the recall order shortly after Narvik was captured. Fortunately for the Allies, the reembarkation was hidden from the eyes of the German fliers on patrol by mist and cloud; clear bombing weather could have converted the vulnerable operation into a catastrophe. As the last troops went aboard ship, a British cruiser also picked up King Haakon and his entourage, who had made their way by rail and automobile across the 1,000-mile length of Norway to the tiny port of Tromso, north of Narvik. The King would maintain a Norwegian government-in-exile in London for the next five years.

After the King's departure, the last organized units of the Norwegian Army surrendered, their position hopeless without aid from the Allies. Hitler's supply of Swedish iron ore was safe, and the Luftwaffe and German Navy had gained invaluable bases for attacks on Britain's maritime life line.

The success of the entire Norwegian campaign had in fact ridden with the Luftwaffe pilots in their cockpits, from the initial capture of the key airfields to the final defeat of the Allied expeditionary forces. The Luftwaffe had shown once more that, in modern warfare, command of the air could give an attacking force the decisive advantage.

Hitler might never have turned his attention to Scandinavia or achieved such a resounding success there had not a curious blunder forced him to postpone his principal aim, the conquest of France. An apparent disaster when it occurred, the blunder in fact helped bring about the Führer's two greatest triumphs.

Hitler, exultant after the smashing victory in Poland in September 1939, had wanted to invade France in November. But worsening weather and the Army's need to regroup caused the attack to be postponed several times. Some bright, clear days in early January, 1940, however, rekindled Hitler's ambitions. A new date for the assault was set: January 17. The German commanders went ahead with preparations, but reluctantly, knowing the Wehrmacht was not yet ready.

Then on January 10 the entire plan was thrown into a cocked hat by a bizarre accident. Fate's agent was a young, ambitious Luftwaffe major named Helmut Reinberger. Delayed in Münster while on a trip to a staff meeting in Cologne, Reinberger decided to avoid a tiring overnight train trip and accept the offer of a ride in a Luftwaffe communications plane. This was strictly against orders. Hermann Göring, the Luftwaffe's chief, had forbidden couriers to carry secret papers by air—and Reinberger's yellow brief case contained the top-secret plan for a key part of the German invasion of France and the Low Countries.

Within minutes after takeoff from Münster's Loddenheide airfield in a small, swift Messerschmitt 108, Reinberger deeply regretted his decision to fly. Wisps of fog soon thickened into a heavy overcast, and a stiff easterly breeze blew the plane some 30 degrees off its southwesterly course. The Rhine River, the key landmark, passed below unseen in the clouds. The pilot, Major Erich Hönmanns, eventually spotted a dark ribbon of water but realized that it was too narrow to be the Rhine. They had lost their way.

By now the cold, damp air was forming ice on the plane's wings and in the carburetor. The engine spluttered and died. Just in time, Hönmanns saw a small field. Narrowly missing a couple of trees on the approach, the Me 108 touched down and bumped to a standstill in a hedge. As the two Germans climbed from the wreckage, shaken but unhurt, an old man appeared. When he told them in French that they had landed at Mechlin in Belgium, Reinberger blanched. The river they had crossed was the Meuse, 50 miles west of Cologne.

"I must burn my papers at once!" Reinberger said frantically. But since neither he nor Hönmanns smoked, they carried no matches. It took time to get the old man to understand what they wanted. He obliged reluctantly with a lighter. But just as Reinberger was getting the documents to catch fire in the stiff breeze, Belgian gendarmes arrived on bicycles and quickly put out the flames.

While being interrogated at the local police station later that day, Reinberger made another desperate attempt to destroy the precious papers by suddenly sweeping them off the table and into a nearby stove. But the police chief reclaimed them from the flames with equal swiftness, although he burned himself in the process.

Now in total despair, the hapless German major tried to snatch the chief's pistol from his holster, but the furious Belgian roughly shoved him into a chair and ordered him to "sit there, and don't move!" Reinberger buried his face in his hands and, half sobbing, explained that he wanted to use the pistol on himself; in Germany, he said, "there will be no pardon for me."

By nightfall the documents, charred around the edges but still legible, were in the hands of the Belgian General Staff, which quickly mobilized the Belgian Army. The Belgians also sent a summary of the papers' contents to the French and British armies in northern France. What the documents outlined was a wheeling movement by the German armies through Belgium and into France—a strategy similar to the one used by the Kaiser's divisions at the beginning of World War I.

When news of Reinberger's misadventure reached Berlin, the repercussions were quick and loud. Hitler upbraided Göring unmercifully for the stupidity of his underlings, Reinberger and Hönmanns, and ordered, "when the courier comes back, have him shot." (Luckily for Reinberger, he was kept safe in a Canadian POW camp for the duration of the War.) Out of all this confusion, however, came a vitally important decision: An entirely new scheme for the invasion would have to be invented. It would, Hitler ordered, be replanned "on a new basis, particularly to be founded on secrecy and surprise."

Responding to Hitler's directive, a brilliant general named Erich von Manstein brought up for the Führer's consideration a plan that a noted historian has called "one of the most inspired blueprints for victory that the military mind has ever conceived." Manstein scrapped the old, predictable idea of making the main attack through Belgium. Instead, as he explained over dinner to Hitler on February 17, 1940, the striking point should be shifted southward to the Ardennes Forest, a hilly, wooded area located where southern Belgium, France and Luxembourg meet. Conventional military wisdom held that tanks could not get through this tumbled woodland, but Manstein insisted it could be done. Not only would the unlikely route of attack gain for the Germans the advantage of surprise, but it would also position them opposite the most lightly defended segment of France's borders. The panzers would hammer through the French defenses near Sedan and drive a wedge all the way to the English Channel, splitting the Anglo-French armies in half.

In this remarkable scheme, the Luftwaffe's job was twofold: first to protect the tanks and armored infantry as they threaded the narrow Ardennes roads, then to lay a carpet of bombs in front of the panzers when they burst into France. As long as the flying artillery created confusion in the enemy ranks, with no pause allowed for recovery, the thrust would succeed.

The attack into northern Belgium and Holland would go ahead, Manstein continued, but largely as a feint, to draw the Allies away from the Ardennes. Army Group B in the north, under Bock, would turn over all but one of its panzer divisions to Army Group A, commanded by Rundstedt, which would deliver the surprise armored blow at Sedan.

Here, then, was the daring, almost reckless kind of plan that Hitler so admired. Manstein's proposal was formally adopted on February 24. The new offensive was aptly code-named *Sichelschnitt,* the "sickle cut." It was during the delay necessary for the two army groups to finish redeploying that Hitler turned north to conquer Norway and Denmark.

Air support for Army Groups A and B was provided by Luftflotten 2 and 3, which together numbered almost 4,000 frontline aircraft, including transports—more than twice as many planes had been assigned to attack Poland. Luftflotte 2 was commanded by a veteran of the Polish campaign, General Kesselring, who took the northern sector of the front. Luftflotte 3 was headed by General Hugo Sperrle, an officer of large girth who loved rich living and high style (he was the only Luftwaffe commander to affect a monocle) but who had a quick and incisive mind. Sperrle's air fleet, assigned to provide the punch for the breakout at Sedan, included Lieutenant General Bruno Loerzer's Fliegerkorps II; Loerzer had shown a marked flair for the close ground support that had helped shatter the Polish Army. Kesselring's force included General von Richthofen's famous Fliegerkorps VIII and General Student's 7th Airborne Division, whose men would again descend from the sky to play a vital part in the conquest of two more small nations, Belgium and the Netherlands.

The Belgian defenses hinged on Fort Eben Emael, a formidable underground labyrinth, bristling with turrets and gunports, that dominated the strategic area where the Meuse River and the Albert Canal intersected. The fort's designers thought they had created a stronghold that was proof against every method of attack. They had not considered assault from the air, however—and that is precisely how the German High Command intended to take Eben Emael, along with three bridges over the Meuse-Albert Canal waterway system that Bock's ground forces would need as they thrust westward through Belgium.

At precisely 4:30 on the morning of May 10, 1940, the first three-plane sections of Ju 52s began taking off into the predawn darkness from two airfields outside Cologne, each transport towing a DFS 230 glider *(pages 56-57)* that was crowded with eight or more of Student's paratroops and their weapons and explosives. Five minutes later all 41 Iron Annies and their gliders were aloft and headed westward toward the German border town of Aachen, their course marked by a variety of seemingly innocuous beacons—a bonfire here, a searchlight there.

Two gliders were prematurely detached from their towplanes by accident and landed in Germany, but the rest of the strange air armada reached the German-Dutch border in about 30 minutes. The gliders were released at roughly 7,500 feet and began their silent, ghostly descent toward the Belgian countryside, three groups of them peeling off toward the bridges, the fourth, of nine gliders, heading for Eben Emael. Glider descents rather than parachute drops had been chosen for these tasks largely because gliders would approach silently, the thundering towplanes having turned back at the German-Dutch border. Gliderborne troops also arrived at the objective in a concentrated group, ready to fight, rather than being scattered as parachutists were.

The well-trained glider pilots of the Eben Emael force landed literally on top of the huge underground fort, on a large grassy field dotted with gun emplacements. The paratroops burst from the gliders with well-rehearsed precision, firing automatic weapons. Nine demolition teams sprinted for their assigned targets, the gun turrets. Grenades lobbed through the embrasures killed the Belgian crews of two 120-millimeter cannon. Nine 75-millimeter guns were blown apart as the Germans popped specially prepared two-pound explosive charges down the barrels. In minutes the glider troops had silenced the fort's topside artillery.

The 700 Belgians inside were in no mood to surrender, however. Their commander ordered Belgian artillery near the fort to open fire on the glider troops, who abruptly went on the defensive, taking cover in the Belgian gun positions they had silenced. They remained under fire for 24 hours, until units of the 151st Infantry Regiment, having advanced from the German border, cracked the Belgian ring around the fort. At 1:15 p.m. on May 11 the Belgians raised a white flag. Eben Emael, the supposedly impregnable bastion, had fallen to 70 German glider troops, who had lost six killed and 20 wounded. A gaping hole

Ju 52 transports sit parked beside the Dutch highway on which they touched down during the Luftwaffe's assault on Holland in May 1940. Other transports fared less well: Unable to land on barricaded airfields, 167 were destroyed, most by antiaircraft fire.

had been punched through the center of Belgium's main defensive line.

Two of the other three sections of glider troops released by their tow-planes over Holland had also done their jobs, capturing the bridges at Veldwezelt and Vroenhaven. By midafternoon Bock's troops, having sped overland from the border, were pouring across the bridges, exploiting the gap created by Eben Emael's capture. Only the bridge at Kanne had been blown by its Belgian defenders, seconds before the gliders touched down. This single failure proved unimportant as units of Army Group B poured across the two bridges that were secure.

Bombers and fighters of Luftflotte 2 swept across the Belgian border soon after the gliders landed. A handful of Belgian and RAF fighter squadrons, flying early Mark I models of the British Hurricane, rose to meet the waves of German aircraft. The Mark I, with a wooden, two-bladed propeller, was 17 miles per hour slower than later Hurricanes, which had metal, three-bladed props. Adolf Galland later wrote that in such outclassed planes "even more experienced pilots could have done little against our new Me 109E. We outstripped them in speed, rate of climb, armament, and above all in flying experience and training."

Galland, who had wangled a transfer to fighters from the Henschel 123 attack planes he had flown in Poland, recounted what happened in his first tangle with these aircraft, on May 12. About "five miles west of Liége," he wrote, "my flight companion and I dived from an altitude of about 12,000 feet on a flight of eight Hurricanes flying 3,000 feet below us." Galland's sporting instincts were outraged when the enemy pilots failed to spot their attackers. " 'Come on, defend yourself!' I thought as soon as I had one of the eight in my gun sight. I closed in without being noticed. 'Someone ought to warn him!' " He fired his Messerschmitt's two machine guns and 20-millimeter cannon. "The poor devil at last noticed what it was all about," he recalled. But it was too late. After a second burst of fire the Hurricane's rudder flew off, then part of a wing.

As his first victim spiraled down, Galland "immediately went after another of the scattered Hurricanes. This one tried to escape by diving, but I was soon on her tail at a distance of 100 yards." The enemy pilot "did a half-roll and disappeared through a hole in the clouds. I did not lose track of him and attacked again from very close quarters. The plane zoomed for a second, stalled, and dived vertically to the ground from a height of 1,500 feet."

Galland took little satisfaction from these first two of the 103 kills he racked up during the War. They had been too easy. The elation of victory, he noted, came only when the German fliers subsequently met newer-model Hurricanes and the Spitfires of the RAF, "when each relentless aerial combat was a question of 'you or me.' "

The Dutch air force put up what defense it could on May 10 with its tiny complement of 52 modern fighters. A group of single-engined Fokker D.XXI monoplanes, built by the Dutch-born Anthony Fokker, who had supplied many of Germany's World War I aircraft, intercepted

A stunning attack on silent wings

The fall of Belgium's Fort Eben Emael to German airborne commandos in 1940 marked the first use of troop-carrying gliders in war—and the fruition of an idea that had been brewing for years.

General Ernst Udet of the Luftwaffe was among the first to envision gliders as modern equivalents of the Trojan horse, able to land troops in stealth behind enemy lines. In 1933, he pushed the development of the DFS 230 (above, right). Made of wood, steel and canvas, the glider was sturdy yet light and could carry eight or more armed troops.

Shortly after the start of the War, General Kurt Student, commander of Germany's airborne forces, organized a detachment of DFS 230s, with an eye to using them in combat. He was vigorously opposed by members of the Army High Command, who regarded gliders as mere transports. Late in 1939, however, Student was given a chance to make his case with Hitler, who put forth a scheme for a nighttime glider attack on Eben Emael in which the gliders would land on top of the underground fort.

Student accepted the proposal immediately—but only if it could be timed for dawn, so his men would have enough light to pick out their targets. Hitler thereupon adjusted the hour of the main Belgian invasion and insisted on a direct glider assault on Eben Emael.

The attack was a stunning success. On May 10, 1940, soldiers led by Lieutenant Rudolph Witzig (below, right) landed on the fort and blew up its big guns. Within 24 hours, Eben Emael, which the Belgians had considered almost invincible, had fallen to the Germans.

The DFS 230 had a wingspan of 72 feet and weighed more than two tons when fully loaded. To reduce drag, it dropped its wheels after takeoff and landed on a wooden nose skid.

Prior to landing, a formation of DFS 230s releases braking parachutes to slow their descent. Some models used rockets to reduce speed for a safer touchdown.

a flight of He 111s shortly after dawn and shot down the German commander's plane. Only minutes later other Fokker D.XXIs sailed into a fleet of 55 Iron Annies carrying paratroops to the airfields around The Hague, the Dutch capital. The Dutch pilots, backed by antiaircraft fire from their compatriots on the ground, shot down or damaged 37 of the transports. These Dutch successes could not be repeated, however, because Kesselring sent waves of He 111s to bomb the enemy airfields. By May 11 only a dozen Fokker D.XXIs were still flyable.

Despite the spirited Dutch resistance, a majority of the 4,000 airborne troops assigned to paralyze the enemy's defenses had landed by noon of May 10. Those assigned to The Hague, arriving battered by the Fokker attacks, failed in their mission to hold the neighboring airfields and to capture the nation's sovereign, Queen Wilhelmina. But the paratroops that were dropped near the main bridges leading across Holland's maze of waterways captured the spans before their surprised guards could blow them up.

The paratroops held on to the all-important bridges in spite of furious counterattacks from Dutch Army units, and by the afternoon of May 12, the 9th Panzer Division had penetrated to the outskirts of Rotterdam, the Netherlands' leading port and a major trading city. But the Dutch forces in Rotterdam would not crack. They were still fighting tenaciously on May 14 when Lieutenant General Rudolf Schmidt warned Colonel Philip Scharroo, the Rotterdam commander, that unless resistance ended quickly, the Germans would resort to any means to break it. "That," Schmidt's note said, "could result in the complete destruction of the city."

Schmidt's was not an idle threat. Hitler had ordered that Rotterdam be bombed into submission if necessary, as Warsaw had been. The 100 He 111s of the 54th Bomber Group, part of Kesselring's Luftflotte 2, had already been assigned the job and were scheduled to take off at about 2 p.m. if the Dutch did not yield. The first wing of 57 planes would be led by Colonel Walter Lackner, and the remaining bombers by Lieutenant Colonel Otto Höhne. Their target: the powerful Dutch force concentrated north of the Maas River, which wound through Rotterdam.

The briefing officers warned the crews that they might see clusters of red Very lights shot from flare pistols rising toward them. If they did, they were not to bomb. The flares would mean that Rotterdam was on the verge of surrender.

Colonel Scharroo took General Schmidt's warning to his superior, the head of the Dutch Army, General Henri Winkelmann. The two Dutch commanders decided to play for time and asked for a parley with the German go-between, an infantry colonel named Dietrich von Choltitz. By 1:50, when Choltitz and Scharroo's emissary, a Captain Bakker, sat down to talk, Lackner's armada was already revving up for takeoff 200 miles away, less than an hour's flying time from Rotterdam.

What followed was a tragedy of failed communications. A message from Schmidt to Luftflotte 2's headquarters—"Attack postponed owing to parley"—was held up by radio interference until 2:15, when Lackner's and Höhne's planes were well on their way. Luftflotte 2's radio operators could not find the radio frequency that was being used by the speeding Heinkels, and by the time Kesselring's headquarters passed the message to the bombers' base near Bremen, which might have made radio contact, it was too late.

In an attempt to head off the bombers, Luftflotte 2's operations officer, Lieutenant Colonel Hans-Jürgen Rieckhoff, leaped into an Me 109 at Münster and flew to Rotterdam. But by the time he got there the bombers had split into their prearranged pattern of attack and were closing in on the Dutch port with their bomb-bay doors open.

On the ground, meanwhile, Colonel Choltitz and his men were frantically firing displays of red Very lights. But though the flares soared high into the sky, they were not bright enough to be noticeable through the swirling smoke and haze drifting over the embattled city. Only one out of the 100 German pilots spotted "two paltry little Very lights." That was Höhne himself, and as he did he shouted to his radio operator to broadcast the code word that signaled, "Abandon the mission and turn back," although his bombardier and those in the next two planes had already pushed their bomb-release buttons.

The rest of Höhne's aircraft aborted their runs, but Lackner's bomber

Fires ravage the Dutch city of Rotterdam following a raid by Luftwaffe bombers on May 14, 1940. The conflagration left nearly 80,000 people homeless.

stream went straight on to unload 97 tons of high explosive on the city. Fanned by a gentle breeze, the fire quickly spread among the old timber houses. Grease from a bombed margarine factory also ignited, spreading the blaze. Three months would pass before the fire's last embers turned cold. First reports claimed that 25,000 people had died in the conflagration. In fact, far fewer—814—actually perished, but the Luftwaffe was blamed for an atrocity, and its reputation for ruthlessness, as well as for overwhelming power, spread, adding to the terror the German aviators inspired in the civilian populations of other nations.

Late on May 14, Dutch General Winkelmann ordered his forces to lay down their arms, and Queen Wilhelmina fled to England aboard a British destroyer. The redoubt of Holland, which the Allied military leaders had hoped could hold out for weeks, had fallen in five days, its natural defensive barriers of rivers and canals breached by the Luftwaffe's airborne assault.

While the glider and paratroop attacks on Belgium and Holland focused Allied attention on the defense of those countries, the assault on France began with the Luftwaffe's now-classic opening gambit: nailing the enemy's air force to the ground. Among the first strikes on the morning of May 11 was a raid by nine Do 17s on an airfield near Vaux. The base was occupied by part of the RAF's Advanced Air Striking Force, sent from England to bolster France's shaky Armée de l'Air.

To achieve surprise, the mission commander, Lieutenant Otto Reimers, led his squadron of fast bombers across the French border at treetop height. As he roared in toward Vaux, Reimers could hardly believe his eyes. There sat a row of blunt-nosed, twin-engined Bristol Blenheim bombers—the best the RAF had in France—neatly lined up wing tip to wing tip as if for a peacetime inspection. The German bombers could hardly miss. Flashes, flames and smoke erupted all along the line of Blenheims, and the 30 aircraft of the RAF's No. 114 Squadron ceased to exist.

Not all of the Luftwaffe's attacks on British and French airfields found such vulnerable targets; many Allied planes were in the air trying to hit the German forces advancing through Belgium. But by the evening of May 12, the Advanced Air Striking Force had lost 63 of its 135 bombers. And the worst was yet to come.

While the bombers of Sperrle's Luftflotte 3 went after airfields and other behind-the-lines targets in France, the seven panzer divisions of Army Group A were stealing through the wooded Eifel district of Germany and the Ardennes regions of northern Luxembourg and southern Belgium. Some French reconnaissance planes spotted these movements on May 11 and 12, and a few of the slow, inadequately armed Potez 63 scouts survived the Me 109s prowling over the advancing tanks to make it back to base. They reported that the Ardennes was alive with motorized columns rumbling toward France. Incredibly, the intelligence officers of the French Ninth Army—a ragtag collection of second-rate reserve divisions holding this supposedly safe sector of the front—refused to believe the pilots' reports. Thus the French lost their only chance of bombing the panzers while they were bunched up and vulnerable on the Ardennes's narrow roads.

The truth burst on the French and British high commands on the morning of May 13, when advance elements of two entire German army corps suddenly appeared on the banks of the Meuse, near Sedan and 40 miles to the north at Dinant. By 7 a.m. waves of Luftwaffe bombers, mostly Do 17s, were thundering over the Meuse to drop high explosives on the French positions guarding the far bank. Succeeding waves followed throughout the morning.

These attacks were only a prelude. Shortly after midday, near Sedan, the pilots of Colonel Walter Sigel's 76th Dive Bomber Group flipped their siren-equipped Stukas into a dive at 12,000 feet. Howling like banshees, the planes fell straight at the terrified French troops. Their 500-pound bombs ripped concrete fortifications out of the ground, overturned artillery pieces and slaughtered the gunners. Colonel Günter Schwartzkopf's 77th Dive Bomber Group simultaneously bombard-

German soldiers mark a French field with a swastika banner to signal Luftwaffe pilots that the area has been occupied by the Wehrmacht. Because of the Army's rapid advance, close ground-to-air coordination was essential to prevent Luftwaffe planes from bombing German troops by mistake.

ed the French fortifications three miles downriver. The concussions were so loud that they temporarily deafened German troops watching the inferno from across the river.

More Stukas followed, and then flights of Dorniers resumed the pounding as Generals Loerzer and von Richthofen threw their combined force of nearly 1,500 aircraft into the battle. Soon the Stukas were back again, refueled, rearmed, circling in the air like hawks and then diving in relays to drop more high explosive on the enemy positions. French fighters tried to get at the Dorniers and Stukas, but they were hopelessly outnumbered. A typical French squadron daily report for May 13 carried the entry: "Between 10 and 11 o'clock a three-plane patrol flying over the area Carignan-Sedan runs into 50 enemy bombers protected by 80 Messerschmitts."

The intensity of the attack by the Stukas was recalled by a sergeant of the 1st Panzer Division who watched from across the Meuse. "Squadron upon squadron rise to a great height, break into line ahead and there, there the first machine hurtles perpendicularly down, followed by the second, third—ten, twelve, aeroplanes there are.

French tanks blocking the German advance in 1940 run a gantlet of attacking Stuka dive bombers. Thick armor protected the tanks from all but direct hits; still, the Stukas could immobilize them by dropping specially designed fragmentation bombs that damaged the vehicles' treads.

"We can see the bombs very clearly," his account continued. "It becomes a regular rain of bombs that whistle down on Sedan and the bunker positions. Each time the explosion is overwhelming, the noise deafening. Everything becomes blended together; along with the howling sirens of the Stukas in their dives, the bombs whistle and crack and burst. A huge blow of annihilation strikes the enemy, and still more squadrons arrive, rise to a great height, and then come down on the same target. We stand and watch what is happening as if hypnotized; down below all hell is let loose!"

This nightmare of bombing shattered the morale of the ill-trained French reservists. "The infantry cowered in their trenches," reported one of the French generals on the scene, "dazed by the crash of bombs and the shriek of the dive bombers." Shortly after 3:00 p.m. the 1st Rifle Regiment of General Heinz Guderian's panzer corps launched rubber rafts and paddled across the Meuse near Sedan, covered by point-blank fire at the French from 88-millimeter guns, the most feared artillery weapon of the War. Downstream at Donchery, German combat engineers threw pontoon bridges across the river to carry Guderian's tanks. Other engineers were busy building bridges at Montharmé and Dinant for Lieutenant General Georg-Hans Reinhardt's and Lieutenant General Hermann Hoth's armored corps. By nightfall on May 13, a tank army unprecedented in warfare for size, mobility and striking power had started across the Meuse and through the gap in the French lines blasted open by the greatest concentration of aerial firepower ever seen.

News of the breakthrough galvanized General Pierre Billotte, commander of the French Army Group I, which was assigned to defend the Sedan area. Billotte immediately telephoned the RAF and the Armée de l'Air, imploring them to bomb the German bridgeheads and especially the pontoon spans across the Meuse as soon as daylight permitted. "Victory or defeat hinges on the destruction of those bridges," Billotte told Air Marshal Arthur Barratt of the Advanced Air Striking Force. But instead of stopping the panzers, the RAF and French planes that responded to Billotte's plea ran head on into what would come to be known as the Massacre of May 14.

The pilots of the first RAF mission of the day, flying 10 obsolete Fairey Battles, single-engined light bombers, somehow avoided the deadly mobile guns of the Luftwaffe *Flakbattalionen* and the roving Messerschmitts that were protecting the panzers, but their bombs missed the narrow, hard-to-hit pontoon bridges.

Next to try were several squadrons of French bombers, spurred on by the two top French Army commanders, Generals Maurice Gamelin and Alphonse Georges, who had become thoroughly alarmed by the German breakout. The Armée de l'Air threw in almost every bomber it had left, from the newest Leo 451 to the oldest Amiot 143, the latter a hopelessly outdated, lumbering machine sardonically called l'Autobus by its crews. The French squadrons found the sky alive with German fighters—mostly from the 2nd and 53rd Fighter Groups, which maintained a constant presence in the area as their squadrons spelled each other in relays. The Messerschmitts pounced on the Amiots and destroyed virtually every plane in one formation. Forty-seven Leo 451s spun into the ground, victims of either fighters or flak. Total French losses were so severe, amounting to nearly half of all the bombers engaged, that the rest of the planned missions were canceled.

In the afternoon it was the RAF's turn again. Air Marshal Barratt sent off 63 Battles and eight Blenheims, escorted by some British Hurricanes and more than 200 French fighters. The bombers, flying low enough to hit the pontoon bridges, were raked from the ground by dozens of German 37-millimeter guns and by the dreaded 88s. When the French and British fighter escorts tried to drive off the Me 109s, squadrons of Me 110s bored in at the low-flying Battles and Blenheims with their twin cannon. Bombers flamed and exploded, littering the lush, green Meuse valley with their wreckage. One British squadron lost 10 of its 11 planes. No. 12 Squadron, already shot to pieces over Belgium, lost four of its last five Blenheims. In all, 40 out of the 71 bombers dispatched were destroyed. Some of their bombs hit Sedan and knocked out some German trucks, but the movement of German reinforcements was halted for only an hour. At dusk Barratt called on RAF Bomber Command, which had maintained its own separate expeditionary force in France, to send out its last 28 Blenheims in a final despairing attempt to get the pontoon bridges; seven were shot down, and the bridges remained intact. The massacre was over, and the British were left without an effective bomber force in France.

The Luftwaffe's awesome performance at the Meuse was of crucial importance in the Battle of France. It enabled the panzer generals—including a relative unknown named Erwin Rommel, who proved to be almost as daring as Guderian himself—to drive a wedge of tanks from Sedan through to the Channel coast with little interference from Allied aircraft. Their great armored thrust sliced in behind the cream of the French divisions and the British, trapping them in Belgium and Flanders and separating them from the remainder of the French Army to the south.

As they dashed across France, the panzers followed a path prepared by relays of Stukas, which flew as many as nine sorties a day each, blocking all Allied attempts to check the German advance. "With bombs and machine guns we attacked the convoys of vehicles," wrote Lieutenant Dietrich Peltz. "The enemy had terrible losses through the work of the Stukas. The enemy fighters appeared less and less, so that the Stukas could fly without fighter cover and could themselves hunt freely. Sometimes it was sheer target practice."

One victim of the Stukas was Colonel Charles de Gaulle. The future President of France commanded a French tank regiment in 1940. Trying to organize his force for an attack on Guderian's corps near Laon, de Gaulle found that "all afternoon the Stukas, swooping out of the sky and returning ceaselessly, attacked our tanks and trucks." Two days later, on May 19, de Gaulle assaulted the German flank with his battered forces, only to be hit again by clouds of Ju 87s. "Till nightfall they were to bombard us," he wrote later, "with formidable effect on our vehicles unable to leave the roads and our artillery out in the open." After this attack, and one more desperate try on May 20, de Gaulle's regiment was forced to retreat; it never again managed to get in position to threaten the advancing panzers.

By May 22, Guderian, having reached the Channel and turned north, was preparing to destroy or capture the British and French armies in Flanders, which had been trapped with their backs to the sea. But the headlong rush of the German tanks was brought to a sudden halt by order of the Führer. Apparently Hitler feared that the fens around Dunkirk might swallow up tanks that would later be needed to complete the destruction of the French armies to the south, which were regrouping in an attempt to save Paris. And anyway Göring, who was determined that his Luftwaffe should not be upstaged by the Army in claiming the laurels of victory, had implored Hitler to "leave the destruction of the enemy surrounded at Dunkirk to me." Hitler granted the request of his favored subordinate.

When Göring ordered his Luftwaffe to the attack, an alarmed Kesselring telephoned him immediately. Kesselring took pains to point out that three weeks of war had reduced some Luftwaffe units by half and that most of the bombers available were based 300 miles from Dunkirk. Göring, whose strength of will had earned him the appellation of "the Iron One," was adamant. Kesselring angrily shouted into the phone, "It won't work!" and banged down the receiver.

The order also astonished Richthofen, who telephoned the Chief of the Luftwaffe's General Staff, Major General Hans Jeschonnek, and told him that unless the panzers got moving again, the British would have time to evacuate the pocket by sea. "No one can seriously believe that we alone can stop them from the air!" he exclaimed.

"You're wrong," replied Jeschonnek. "The Iron One believes it. What's more, the Führer wishes to spare the British too crushing a defeat!"

"Yet we are to go all out all the same," said Richthofen, incredulous.

"Quite so. With all the forces at your command."

Göring committed some 500 fighters and 300 bombers to the destruction of the British Expeditionary Force and the French army trapped with it. On paper, this was a powerful concentration of aircraft. But after two weeks of intensive action, the wear and tear on men and machines had taken its toll. Furthermore, the Luftwaffe for the first time was facing an equal opponent. At Dunkirk, the RAF would be operating from its home bases in Southern England rather than from the makeshift airfields it had used in France. Moreover, the RAF committed to the battle its newest and best fighter, the Spitfire, which had been held in reserve until now.

As the evacuation of the trapped Allied force began on May 27,

Luftwaffe planes furiously attacked the troops huddling on Dunkirk's beaches—and were themselves whipsawed by formations of agile Spits. Air Vice Marshal Sir Keith Park, commanding the RAF fighters in southern England, ordered his planes into standing patrols. Thirty-two squadrons took turns flying watches of 40 minutes each over the coast near Dunkirk, trying to provide air protection for the men on the beaches below. Large German formations still got through, but they were made to pay for their successes. "The enemy fighters pounced on our tightly knit formations with the fury of maniacs," recalled German bomber pilot Major Werner Kreipe. On that first day of the Dunkirk air battles Fliegerkorps II suffered losses that exceeded those of the previous 10 days of fighting.

Four days of cloudy weather that grounded the Luftwaffe gave the Allies a heaven-sent breather. When the sun reemerged on June 1, Fliegerkorps II returned to the attack—only to find the Spitfires back on guard. The RAF never really achieved air superiority over Dunkirk, but it did blunt the Luftwaffe's attacks so effectively that by June 4, the last day of the evacuation, 338,226 British and French soldiers had escaped to England. Hitler seemed unperturbed by the salvation of the enemy armies. England, he believed, would soon come to its senses, perceive that the situation was hopeless and seek to negotiate a peace with Germany. He treated the Dunkirk affair as a great victory and ordered church bells rung all over Germany for three days.

But Dunkirk had in fact been the Luftwaffe's first setback—at a cost of some 300 dead aviators—and it clearly indicated to Kesselring and the other Luftwaffe generals that their vain and willful chief, Göring, was quite capable of committing the air force to foolhardy operations. He would do so again, very soon.　～～

Four German Me 110s overfly Paris after the French surrender on June 22, 1940. The mixture of relentless Luftwaffe tactical strikes and swift panzer thrusts enabled Germany to conquer its old enemy in only six weeks.

Life at rustic forward bases

After the fall of France in June 1940, Luftwaffe units began moving to forward bases along the Channel to be within striking distance of England. Scattered around the countryside, the strips were mostly primitive affairs; the French had concentrated on fields in the east to protect their border with Germany. While workers went about the task of improving the bases, pilots and crews amused themselves on leave on sunny Channel beaches or strolled along boulevards where shopkeepers had hastily replaced signs advertising "English Spoken Here" with newly printed placards: *"Man Spricht Deutsch."*

Their idyll was short-lived. On July 16, Hitler issued his top-secret order for the invasion of Great Britain. Some 2,600 aircraft, including 1,480 bombers and 980 fighters, were now in position at the bases, and the air battle was soon under way. So accustomed did pilots become to flying missions across the Channel that for many it was "just like going to the office in the morning and coming home in the evening." Yet all knew that they could die any day. "Those of us who returned from a combat mission," remembered an Me 109 pilot, "were able to enjoy a few more hours of life, and we let ourselves go so as to enjoy life's pleasures to the fullest. At the slightest excuse we gambled, drank, laughed, talked shop or acted the fool."

To relieve tensions and lift spirits, pilots were taken by bus to the beaches. At one base, a Ju 52 called "the vitamin bomber," flew to Guernsey, a British Channel island occupied by the Germans, for tomatoes, fresh vegetables, grapes, cigarettes and whiskey. The vegetables and fruit came as a welcome treat to men fed up with canned food. German films were screened regularly, and from loudspeakers around the bases came music (the same speakers would flash word of upcoming raids against England). Radios brought news from Germany. And then there were the women; the uniformed *Helferinnen vom Dienst* (female helpers of the service) operated the telephone and telegraph and performed clerical duties, but their presence on the bases—and their obliging natures—did as much as anything to bolster Luftwaffe morale.

Ignoring a Dornier 17 bomber on the edge of their wheat field, a French couple harvests the 1940 crop. The plane belonged to a unit of the Luftwaffe's Air Fleet 2 based in Arras, 100 miles north of Paris.

A Luftwaffe mechanic shaves at a makeshift table beside his tent at a forward airfield in France. Pilots were usually put up in barracks.

At a muddy forward airfield that is still lacking the basic equipment with which to service its aircraft, burly Luftwaffe crew members haul bombs on their shoulders toward a waiting bomber.

Heinkel 111 bombers lie hidden beneath the trees at the edge of an airstrip in western France. The men who flew them got one day off between missions, which irritated the ground crews, who had to work all the time.

"Special workers"—the German euphemism for forced labor—finish work on a bomber field in northwestern France in preparation for the bombing of England.

Luftwaffe ground-crew members arm a Heinkel 111 bomber concealed underneath a camouflage screen. The plane could carry a 5,500-pound load of bombs.

An officer briefs bomber crews before a sortie over Britain in August 1940. "It's really just so much routine," a pilot said of such sessions: "Most of the time we know our target before the chief says a word."

German fliers scramble toward their He 111 for a cross-Channel mission in 1940. By midsummer, raids on Britain had become so frequent that air crews joked they would soon need police in the air to regulate traffic.

Dornier 17 bombers warm up their engines at a French air base prior to an attack on English coastal radar stations and fighter bases.

3

A surprise for Göring's eagles

When the French government's delegation gathered in the old railway car parked in the Forest of Compiègne on the warm afternoon of June 21, 1940, to listen to the German terms of surrender, Adolf Hitler stayed only to hear the brief preamble. Then, in a calculated insult to vanquished France, the Führer and his retinue abruptly left the car—the same one in which imperial Germany had surrendered to the Allies in 1918—and strode triumphantly toward their waiting automobiles. At Hitler's side as he passed a German guard of honor and military band was Hermann Göring, resplendent in a sky blue uniform. Like Hitler, Göring gloated over the stunning defeat handed to the French, and he basked in the glories of his Luftwaffe, now invincible from the Arctic Circle to the Bay of Biscay.

Only Britain was standing openly opposed to German designs in Europe, but Hitler clung to the belief that the British—whom he considered to be good Aryans like the Germans—would realize the hopelessness of their position and sue for peace. Churchill had other ideas, however, and vowed that Britain would fight on. "We shall never surrender," he said, and when the tattered British Expeditionary Force had returned from Dunkirk, Britain prepared for the German invasion. Church bells were stilled, to be sounded only when enemy landing craft or paratroopers were sighted. Miles of barbed wire were strung along the beaches. Signposts giving directions and distances to villages were uprooted to make it difficult for Germans to find their way. Old cars were junked in open fields to wreck infantry-laden gliders. The elderly and the infirm joined the Home Guard, some armed with 1914 Lee-Enfield rifles, others with fowling pieces and even pitchforks.

In the face of this British defiance, Hitler retired to a Black Forest retreat to confer with his admirals and generals about what to do next. The Führer finally decided that planning for an invasion should be started, a prospect that filled all present with misgivings. Germany had no experience in amphibious warfare, no special landing craft, no aircraft carriers, and half its destroyer fleet had been lost during the Norwegian campaign. Moreover, the earliest practical date for Operation *Sea*

A Messerschmitt 110 sweeps along the cliffs of Dover during the Luftwaffe's campaign to prepare the way for an invasion of Britain in 1940. Full-scale air attacks began on August 13, when 485 bomber and 1,000 fighter sorties were launched across the Channel.

Lion, as the invasion was code-named, was mid-September, a time when the Channel was usually whipped into choppiness.

Of one thing Hitler's officers were certain: *Sea Lion* stood no chance at all unless the Luftwaffe could gain absolute mastery of the air over the Channel and southern England. Göring, left smarting by the Luftwaffe's failure to eradicate the British Expeditionary Force at Dunkirk, assured Hitler that the RAF would be brought to its knees within six weeks so that *Sea Lion* could proceed. Since shipping was vital to the island British, Göring reasoned, the RAF would use everything it had to protect the convoys steaming to and fro through the narrow English Channel. German bombers would lure the RAF Fighter Command into battle over the convoys—and the RAF would be destroyed by the Luftwaffe.

With the Führer's blessing, Göring arrayed his forces for the onslaught. The sector reaching from the Netherlands to France's Seine River belonged to Albert Kesselring, now promoted to field marshal, and his Luftflotte 2. Field Marshal Hugo Sperrle commanded Luftflotte 3; his sector stretched south of the Seine. Far to the north, in Stavanger, Norway, was General Hans-Jürgen Stumpff's Luftflotte 5.

Stumpff's force was relatively small, and the distance from Norway to England would be stretching the range of his bombers. So the burden of combat would fall to Luftflotten 2 and 3. Between them they could field 828 twin-engined medium bombers, 280 Stuka dive bombers, 760 Messerschmitt 109 single-engined fighters, 220 Me 110 twin-engined fighters and 140 reconnaissance aircraft. Against this force the British, who had suffered heavy losses in the Battle of France, could muster only 603 Hurricanes and Spitfires.

Göring chose Colonel Johannes Fink to direct the Channel fighting. Fink, a 50-year-old veteran airman, commanded *Kampfgeschwader 2* and still flew missions at the head of this bomber group of some 100 planes. Fink appointed another grizzled air warrior, 48-year-old Colonel Theo Osterkamp, to head the fighter unit. Known affectionately as Onkel Theo, Osterkamp had shot down 32 Allied fighters during World War I and for his bravery had been awarded the Pour le Mérite— the coveted Blue Max.

The fighters and bombers that would take part in the Channel battles had been refurbished after the French campaign and were flown in from maintenance depots to their operational fields. Some of the Luftwaffe fighters were based near Calais, only 22 miles across the Channel from Dover; the others were scattered across airfields on the Cherbourg peninsula where the pilots faced some 80 miles of open water before reaching land. The bombers, with a greater operational radius, were stationed on fields farther inland.

Göring's instructions to Fink and the Luftflotte commanders were clear: They must close the Channel to British shipping, which consisted largely of coastal steamers and colliers—their coal was badly needed to warm British homes and fire industrial furnaces—coming from the north. In the process, they were expected to drive the defending British fighter force from the skies and clear the way for the invasion.

Fink and the others worked out the tactical plan to draw the RAF into battle. German radar would pick out the convoys as they started down the Channel. The bombers would take to the air and rendezvous with the escorting fighters at altitudes ranging from 10,000 to 17,000 feet, depending on cloud cover. Then the Luftwaffe planes would streak across the Channel, bomb the ships and attack the RAF fighters that rose to defend them.

The battle for the Channel opened in earnest on the rainswept morning of Wednesday, July 10, 1940. Shortly after dawn, one of Kesselring's slender Dornier 17 reconnaissance planes flew through broken clouds and was within sight of Yarmouth when a patrolling Spitfire sliced down and opened fire at close range. The Dornier pilot rammed his throttles forward and escaped into the enveloping gray of a nearby cloud.

This lone reconnaissance plane was quickly followed by more than 50 Do 17s and Me 109s, sent up by Kesselring's Luftflotte 2. The marauding planes broke into the clear over the Channel and headed for a convoy that was approaching Yarmouth. The pilots were eager for a challenge from the British. It came quickly, and the outcome was hardly what the Germans had in mind. Eight Spitfires, flying routine dawn patrol from their forward base at Manston, on the Thames estuary, fell upon the raiders; in the confused melee that followed a Spitfire pumped a three-second machine-gun burst into a Dornier and sent it plunging into the sea; then two Me 109s rammed each other and followed the Dornier down. The German pilots broke off the battle, and the convoy steamed on unharmed.

German bombers struck at other isolated British convoys that morning, sinking a small freighter but losing an escorting Me 109 to the guns of a nimble Spitfire. Then, at one o'clock that afternoon, still keeping to the plan, Fink called on planes from Luftflotte 2 to attack another convoy steaming through the Strait of Dover. An armada of 20 Do 17s, 20 Me 109s and 30 twin-engined Me 110 fighters was dispatched to the Channel.

As the 70 aircraft approached the convoy, the Luftwaffe fighter commander, Captain Hannes Trautloft—a tough veteran of aerial combat over Spain and France—spotted six Hawker Hurricanes climbing fast. Trautloft, sure that the Hurricanes would soon have company, kept his formations intact. Minutes later, the first group of British defenders was joined by some 30 Spitfires and Hurricanes. The Me 110 pilots watched warily while a formation of Spitfires climbed above them. The German airmen had seen this before, over Dunkirk, and they knew that dueling with the agile, eight-gunned Spitfires in the heavy, unwieldy 110s was asking for trouble. The 110s joined in a protective circle, each fighter chasing the tail of another.

The Spitfires let the 110s circle uselessly while they and the Hurricanes bored in for the bombers, knocking three 109s out of the

Photographed from the cockpit of a Luftwaffe fighter plane above the cliffs of Dover, an RAF Hurricane careens through the air after losing a wing (upper right) to a burst of German fire. The pilot (top) has already bailed out, and his parachute is blossoming over his head.

sky en route. Then Lieutenant Walter Oesau, another veteran of the Spanish fighting, destroyed two Spitfires within as many minutes; Oesau was on the tail of a third Spitfire, firing, when the British fighter flew full tilt into a 109 and touched off a spectacular explosion. The engagement was broken off only when the German fighters, running short on fuel, had to head for home.

The next day, July 11, it was the turn of the eager pilots of Sperrle's Luftflotte 3 to go into action. Especially keen were the airmen of Fliegerkorps VIII, who would be given their first opportunity to unleash their Ju 87 Stuka dive bombers against British shipping. The unit's feisty commander, General Wolfram von Richthofen, had seen his Stukas strike terror and confusion among the enemy ever since their introduction to modern warfare in Spain, and he was sure they would do likewise in the battle against England.

Shortly after 8 a.m.—not long after the rear gunner of a Do 17 reconnaissance plane had downed an attacking RAF Hurricane—10 of Richthofen's Stukas, escorted by 20 Me 109s, prepared to hurl themselves on a small convoy hugging the English coast. But the attack was disrupted by a trio of Hurricanes that disregarded the odds and waded into the swarm of German aircraft. A 109 sent one British fighter into the Channel, then the Stukas screamed down toward the plodding ships below—only to be set upon by six newly arrived Spitfires. The British planes in turn were bounced by the 109s, diving down from the glare of the sun. Two of the Spitfires were destroyed, but not before the Stukas were forced to scatter, leaving the convoy unharmed.

Thick clouds gathered over the Channel later in the morning, and it was not until early afternoon that Richthofen's pilots again were aloft, this time with 15 Ju 87s and an escort of 40 Me 110s. Their destination was Portland, one of Britain's largest ports, and the farthest west the Luftwaffe had so far tried to penetrate. The German pilots expected the British to put up a maximum effort to defend the ships in the harbor, and they were puzzled when only six Hurricanes based at nearby Tangmere rose to meet the challenge. The defenders swept down from superior altitude, bypassing the sluggish 110s to whipsaw the Stukas, two of which were knocked out of the sky. Once again, the attackers dispersed without inflicting serious damage on their intended targets.

At 6 p.m. a dozen He 111s escorted by a like number of Me 110s fought their way through to Portland and managed to unload their bombs on the shipping and the docks, but on the way home several were shot down over the Channel by determined Hurricane pilots.

Fink and Osterkamp were undismayed. For the first few days of the battle they were content merely to probe British defenses. The RAF was indeed rising to meet the challenge to British shipping, but in far smaller numbers than the two commanders had anticipated. In fact, so few British fighters were responding to the Luftwaffe's challenge that some of the Germans believed the RAF was already running out of Spitfires and Hurricanes.

The fact is that the commitment of only small numbers of fighters to protect shipping was a deliberate policy of Air Chief Marshal Sir Hugh Dowding, Commander in Chief of the RAF's Fighter Command. Dowding was determined to husband his fighters against the worse days to come, and he had decreed that coastal convoys would receive minimum fighter protection, or no cover at all if it came to that. Certain that the Luftwaffe would soon be attacking targets in Britain itself, Dowding had no intention of squandering his precious fighters to protect coal shipments that could as readily be dispatched by rail (as indeed they eventually were).

Even in their small numbers the British continued to inflict heavy losses on the Germans. This was all too clear to Trautloft, whose fighter unit began the battle with 40 Me 109s and within a week of fighting could muster only 15 serviceable planes. But Trautloft was hardly out of action. On July 19, reinforced with new fighters and fresh pilots, he took to the air at the head of 25 Me 109s, and after an uneventful bomber escort mission he went looking for a fight.

The earphones in Trautloft's leather helmet crackled, then he heard the familiar voice of his wingman: "Far below us, on the right, exactly over the coast, several Indians." Trautloft looked down and saw nine British single-engined planes south of the seaside town of Folkestone "flying closely together, almost as though they were on parade."

They were Boulton-Paul Defiants of the RAF's No. 141 Squadron, sent south from Scotland 10 days earlier. The Defiant was a peculiar fighter, armed with four .303-caliber machine guns mounted in a manned turret behind the cockpit. But the craft had no forward-firing guns, and wags in the RAF observed that the Defiant had to fly past a German plane before attacking it.

Trautloft scanned the sky above to make sure the Defiants were not acting as decoys for high-flying Spitfires. Then, at 1:43 p.m., he radioed for the attack to begin. He picked a Defiant at the end of the follow-the-leader formation, closed the range to 150 yards and opened fire with his two 20-millimeter cannon and twin machine guns. The Defiant turrets swiveled and the British gunners opened up at the same time. But Trautloft bored in through the tracers. Later, he gave a graphic description of the experience: "A fantastic fireworks. Shots ring to my right and left. Somewhere in my Messerschmitt I feel a strong blow and hear a heavy rumbling, but the opponent has to go! I see a thin line of smoke under his fuselage, then suddenly the enemy plane is one red ball of fire rushing downward." Trautloft turned away to seek another victim, but all he saw were Defiants plunging and spinning out of control.

His elation was cut short when the smell of hot oil filled the cockpit and the radiator-temperature-gauge needle swung to the right, nudging the red. His engine disabled, Trautloft wheeled for France, followed by another Me 109 with similar problems. Trautloft's faltering plane reached the French coast when he was down to 600 feet. He skimmed over the cliffs to make a rough landing at his airfield near the village of St.-Inglevert.

Trautloft and his men had done good work that day. Six of the nine Defiants were blown out of the sky; a seventh landed back at Hawkinge so badly damaged it never flew again. No. 141 Squadron had ceased to exist as a fighting unit, and the Defiants were withdrawn from the RAF line of battle.

As the Channel battle raged on, its ferocity increased. Shortly before noon on July 25 Fink stepped outside his seaside command post at Cap Gris-Nez, close to Calais, and trained powerful binoculars on a 21-ship British convoy sailing down the Channel. Overhead an entire wing of 40 of Kesselring's Me 109s gathered in the brilliant sky, dropped down almost to the wave tops and whipped across the Channel to support a Stuka attack on the strung-out ships.

The low-flying Messerschmitts drew Spitfires down to their level to dogfight. But a 109 pilot miscalculated his firing approach, dived too steeply and pulled up too late; his fighter cartwheeled into the sea. Both the German and the British fighters quickly exhausted their fuel and turned for home to refuel and rearm. This was the moment the Stukas had been waiting for: Sixty of them fell on the naked convoy and sent five ships to the bottom. But there were still plenty of ships afloat, and the battle continued to rage throughout the afternoon. Successive waves of Spitfires, Hurricanes, Stukas, Dorniers, Ju 88s and Me 109s converged over the convoy. When the fighting was over another six ships lay crippled in the water, and three of these were finished off by German torpedo boats. Sixteen Luftwaffe raiders lay at the bottom of the Channel, but so did seven of Dowding's fighters.

Three days later, the battle was joined by Major Werner Mölders, the new commander of *Jagdgeschwader 51,* a group of some 100 fighters. Mölders was only 28, but his serious demeanor had earned him the nickname Daddy. He had shot down 14 Republican planes during the Spanish Civil War and his bag during the Battle of France had amounted to 25 French and British aircraft—despite the fact that he suffered from chronic airsickness. Shot down himself on June 5 by a French Dewoitine fighter, Mölders had spent a short time as a French prisoner of war before repatriation. Mölders was eager for action. He had been out of combat for more than seven weeks, watching as other pilots were piling up victory after victory in the Channel battle.

On Sunday afternoon, Mölders led a wing of more than 30 of his Me 109s in a sweep north of Dover, hoping that his airsickness would not interfere with his first engagement with the RAF over its home ground. Mölders and his comrades bounced some low-flying Spitfires, one of which Mölders shot down in flames. As he later recalled: "Now I found myself in the middle of a clump of Englishmen and they were very angry at me. They all rushed at me, and that was my good luck. As they all tried to earn cheap laurels at the expense of one German, they got in one another's way."

Mölders extricated himself from the aerial entanglement and fastened on the tail of a Spitfire he hoped would become his 27th victim of the War. Unfortunately for Mölders he had picked the leader of No. 74 Squadron, Adolph Gysbert "Sailor" Malan, a burly 30-year-old South African who was on his way to 35 kills. Malan shot down a Messerschmitt before realizing that Mölders was on his tail. Then he racked his Spitfire around in a tight turn, and Mölders watched Malan's plane disappear from his sights. Malan swooped around behind Mölders' Me 109 and opened up with his eight Browning machine guns. Points of fire danced all over the German fighter. "Bullets bespattered my aircraft," Mölders recalled. "The radiator and the fuel tank were badly shot up and I had to make a getaway as quickly as possible." He half-rolled and dived away, managing to reach the French coast with an overheated, misfiring engine. The landing gear would not descend and Mölders' plane landed on its belly in a long, sliding sprawl in an open field.

For all its ferocity, the battle over the Channel was fought with a

A pilot's-eye view of the Me 109

The cockpit of an Me 109 was a cramped but efficient battle station. With the canopy closed, a pilot scarcely had room to turn his head, but his controls and instruments were ready at hand. He was adequately armed to stand off the best of the Allies' planes. Still, the Messerschmitt was fully 10 years old as it rounded out its fighting career, and it did not have many of the refinements introduced on Axis and Allied warplanes of later design.

The flying controls were, for the most part, similar to those of other fighters, old or new. A push-pull motion on the control column *(30 on the keyed diagram included below)* operated the elevators, which raised and lowered the nose, while a sideways motion worked the ailerons; foot pedals with straps to hold the feet in place *(29)* moved the rudder. A trimming device—a wheel *(33)* that plied tabs on the elevators—enabled the pilot to fine-tune the pitch of the aircraft, and a separate hand-wheel *(32)* allowed him to raise and lower the flaps.

The instrument panel, although arranged differently from the T configuration standardized on Allied planes, was logical and easy to follow. Flight instruments—altimeter *(6)*, compass *(7)*, turn-and-bank and air-speed indicators *(11, 10)*—were grouped on a protective antishock panel beneath the front windshield. Engine-readout dials *(8, 13, 14, 16, 17, 25, 26, 27)*, a radio *(24)* and landing gear controls *(18, 19, 28)* were clustered below. Notably missing were such instruments as the gyrocompass and the artificial horizon. As a result the Me 109 was ill equipped for flying under instrument conditions.

1. REFLECTOR GUN SIGHT
2. FLIGHT-RESTRICTION CARD
3. CLOCK
4. LIGHT
5. IGNITION SWITCH
6. ALTIMETER
7. COMPASS
8. MANIFOLD-PRESSURE GAUGE
9. COMPASS-DEVIATION CARD
10. AIR-SPEED INDICATOR
11. TURN-AND-BANK INDICATOR
12. PROPELLER-PITCH CONTROL
13. TACHOMETER
14. PROPELLER-PITCH INDICATOR
15. ULTRAVIOLET LAMP
16. RHEOSTAT
17. OIL-PRESSURE GAUGE
18. LANDING GEAR INDICATOR
19. LANDING GEAR SELECTOR
20. FILTER-PUMP CONTROL
21. FUEL-MIXTURE CONTROL
22. THROTTLE
23. FUEL COCK
24. RADIO
25. FUEL GAUGE
26. OIL-TEMPERATURE GAUGE
27. RADIATOR-TEMPERATURE GAUGE
28. EMERGENCY LANDING GEAR LEVER
29. RUDDER PEDALS
30. CONTROL COLUMN
31. OXYGEN APPARATUS
32. FLAP WHEEL
33. TRIM WHEEL

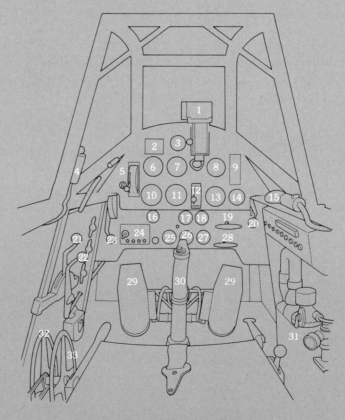

The cockpit of the Me 109 was enclosed by a cumbersome hood that had to be raised to starboard, making bailout difficult.

surprising amount of old-fashioned chivalry. In one action, a pair of Me 109 pilots shot Pilot Officer John Simpson's Hurricane to pieces off the coast of southern England; Simpson, wounded in the foot, went over the side at 16,000 feet and pulled the rip cord. Strong winds drove him toward land, and as he drifted helplessly to earth the British pilot saw that one of the German fliers was circling him. Simpson knew the rules: Pilots who parachuted over their own territory were considered fair game—they would land and fly again. The German pilot tightened his circle until Simpson could make out the details of the other's face. The Britisher braced himself for the brief burst of machine-gun and cannon fire that would end his life, but the German pilot waved, and suddenly the Messerschmitt was gone. Simpson landed safely in a cucumber patch.

On another occasion, Luftwaffe pilot Erich Rudorffer dueled unsuccessfully with some Hurricanes over Dover, then broke off combat and headed his Me 109 back across the Channel. He spotted a Hurricane flying in the opposite direction trailing a long plume of white smoke. "I flew up alongside him," Rudorffer recalled after the War, "and escorted him all the way to England and then waved good-by. A few weeks later the same thing happened to me. That would never have happened in Russia—never."

By the end of July, Hitler was growing impatient with the Luftwaffe's lack of progress. On August 1, from his aerie above Berchtesgaden, he issued his Directive No. 17 for the Conduct of the War: "In order to establish the conditions necessary for the final conquest of England, I intend to continue the air and naval war against the English homeland more intensively than heretofore." The Luftwaffe was specifically charged with overcoming the RAF "with all means at its disposal and as soon as possible." This stepped-up aerial warfare could commence "on or after August 6."

On the same day Göring summoned his Luftwaffe commanders to a conference at The Hague, capital of the Netherlands. "Everybody with a name or a rank worth mentioning was there," Theo Osterkamp recalled later. "The weather was perfect so the party took place in the garden. The 'Iron One' appeared in a new white ceremonial uniform."

Göring's address to the others was filled with bombast. "The Führer," he said, "has ordered me to crush Britain with my Luftwaffe. By delivering a series of very heavy blows I plan to have this enemy, whose morale is already at its lowest, down on his knees in the nearest future so that our troops can land on the island without any risk."

It was clear that the Luftwaffe's previous strategy had been a failure. The war over the Channel had cost 286 German planes, including 105 fighters, while the British had lost 148 Spitfires and Hurricanes. The RAF was proving to be a far tougher opponent than the Luftwaffe had anticipated, and German intelligence had consistently underestimated the rate of British fighter production. In consequence, the output of

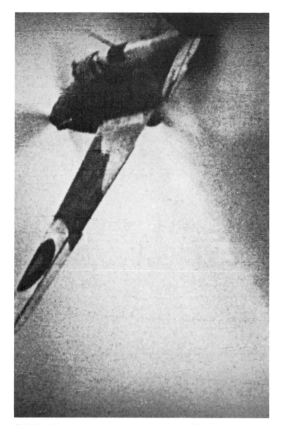

Riddled by bullets from a pursuing Me 109, a Hurricane fighter spirals out of control over southern England in September 1940. The picture was taken by automatic cameras installed in the German plane to record the combat for later use in confirming victories and training cadets.

Me 109s continued at a leisurely peacetime pace. In June 1940, only 164 Me 109s rolled off the lines of the main Messerschmitt factory at Augsburg, while the British turned out 446 Hurricanes and Spitfires. During July, when the fighting—and the losses—intensified, the RAF received another 496 fighters; the Luftwaffe got only 220. The Germans were being outproduced by more than 2 to 1.

Osterkamp informed Göring that he believed that RAF Fighter Command could field 11 new fighter squadrons, all equipped with Spitfires. Göring replied angrily: "This is nonsense! Our information is excellent, and I am perfectly aware of the situation. The Messerschmitt is much better than the Spitfire because the British are too cowardly to engage your fighters."

Osterkamp patiently responded that when British fighters had avoided combat with the German fighters, it was to concentrate instead on attacking bombers.

"That's the same thing!" Göring shouted.

On August 5, Göring summoned Kesselring, Sperrle, Stumpff and Field Marshal Erhard Milch, his chief deputy, to Karinhall, Göring's opulent manor house 40 miles northeast of Berlin. This time, the Reich Marshal was in an expansive mood, offering brandy and cigars all around. In rooms hung with lush tapestries and gilt-framed oils of nudes, the leading Luftwaffe commanders thrashed over the means by which the Führer's latest directive could be carried out. Sperrle wanted to concentrate on bombing ports and harbors, while Kesselring proposed one overwhelming attack on London that would draw the RAF into the air for a battle of annihilation. Göring pointed out that Hitler specifically forbade attacks on ports and harbors in southern England because they would be needed for *Sea Lion,* and that mounting terror attacks on London and other large cities was an option that required direct orders from the Führer himself.

Göring made the final decision. The Luftwaffe would return to the basic tactic that had been so successful in Poland and in France: Destroy the enemy's air force on the ground—or at least wipe out his most important fighter bases—while knocking down any planes that manage to get airborne. It was an ambitious plan. On the first day of the new assault, Luftwaffe bombers, heavily escorted by fighters, would move inland from the Channel to attack Fighter Command's forward bases. During the second day airfields in the London area would be hit with saturation bombing; these same inner fields guarding the heart of London would be assaulted again on day three. By the fourth day Fighter Command should be finished as an effective force. With air supremacy established, the Luftwaffe could then wreck the rest of the Royal Air Force—its bomber fields and Coastal Command installations—in time for *Sea Lion* to be launched unopposed from the air on September 15, just six weeks away.

To set a date for the start of the new aerial offensive, Göring called on his meteorologists for long-range weather forecasts. Their predictions indicated that August 10 would be propitious for the first blow, and Göring gave the assault's opening day the code name *Adlertag,* or Eagle Day. If all went according to plan, the invasion of Britain could begin as scheduled.

Along the French coast, nearly 250,000 German troops stood in readiness for the cross-Channel assault. Now it was up to the Luftwaffe to clear the skies of British defenders. Kesselring and Sperrle could throw some 2,000 aircraft into the battle, including 929 fighters, 875 medium bombers and 316 Stukas. Ranged against this German aerial armada were about 700 operational Spitfires and Hurricanes; nearly half of the pilots who would fly these fighters into battle were replacements who had never flown against the enemy.

As Eagle Day came nearer, long-range Focke-Wulf 200 weather-reconnaissance planes brought disappointing news from over the Atlantic. Bad weather was sweeping in toward the Channel. Göring reluctantly postponed Eagle Day until August 13. At the same time, he ordered a preliminary assault against some key RAF bases and the chain of radar stations strung along England's southern and eastern coasts. Only recently had the Germans learned that these installations were providing the RAF with advance notice of approaching Luftwaffe formations; their destruction was vital to the success of the coming offensive.

Among the attackers from Kesselring's Luftflotte 2 was a new unit, Experimental Group 210, commanded by 30-year-old Captain Walter Rubensdörffer. The group's three squadrons of Me 109s and 110s had been modified to carry bombs of up to 1,000 pounds. For several weeks these special fighter-bombers had been hitting at British shipping; now their targets were the spindly radar towers along the coast.

Rubensdörffer's squadrons headed out over the Channel shortly before 9 a.m. on August 12. As they neared the coastline they split up and streaked for their separate objectives, raining bombs on the radar stations at Dover, Rye, Pevensey and the Kentish town of Dunkirk. Then, untouched by enemy fire, the planes flew back to Calais to refuel and rearm. They had knocked three of the radar stations out of action, though none of the 350-foot steel masts had been toppled.

In another attack that day, Sperrle sent Stukas and twin-engined Ju 88s, protected by fighter escorts, against Portsmouth harbor on England's south coast and against the hilltop radar station at Ventnor on the nearby Isle of Wight. Fifteen Ju 88s flew unmolested over the island and battered Ventnor with eight tons of bombs; Ventnor's radar equipment would be off the air for the next 11 days.

The second part of Göring's plan was begun that afternoon when Fink—again leading his own group of Do 17s—joined Experimental Group 210 in a strike against the large Fighter Command base at Manston. Lieutenant Martin Lutz of the Experimental Group took his squadron of Me 110s down to 1,000 feet to skip their bombs across the field where Spitfire pilots were frantically trying to scramble. "The fighters were all lined up," Lutz recalled. "Our bombs fell right among them."

The 350-foot-tall masts of Britain's Dover radar station rise behind two Me 109s in a 1940 German photograph taken with a high-power lens from across the Channel. The masts were so difficult to hit in bomb runs that not a single one was felled during an all-out Luftwaffe attack on four stations on August 12, 1940.

Other Luftwaffe groups continued to press attacks on RAF forward airfields, including Lympne and Hawkinge—on the Channel coast opposite Calais—until early evening. It all seemed like a great victory to the German commanders. But the British were already putting three of the stricken radar stations back in operation; they would be warmed up and ready for the morrow, Eagle Day.

Early on the morning of August 13 the Luftwaffe Chief of Staff, General Hans Jeschonnek, looked over the latest weather forecast, which promised good bombing over southern England. Then a Dornier 17 weather-reconnaissance plane sent out just before dawn returned to France, and the pilot reported that the weather was deteriorating; Eagle Day promised to open with mist and drizzle over all of the southeastern counties. Jeschonnek got on the telephone and reported to Göring, who immediately postponed the operation until midafternoon. His order went out to all of Sperrle's groups—but it failed to reach Fink at his base at Arras.

Shortly after 5 a.m. Fink eased into the pilot's seat of his worn Do 17 and took off across the Channel at the head of 73 other Dornier bombers bound for the RAF field at Eastchurch on the south bank of the Thames estuary. Fink could see a wing of more than 30 Me 110s forming up in the distance to escort them to the target. Leading the fighters was an air warrior in whom Fink had the greatest confidence, another "old crock" like himself, Lieutenant Colonel Joachim Huth, who had lost a leg during World War I.

Not long after takeoff, Huth and the other Me 110 pilots received a recall order. Again, the order did not reach Fink, whose bombers continued to drone toward England. Huth tried to raise Fink on the radio but could not reach him; the Luftwaffe Signals Service had failed to provide the Dorniers with the right crystals for their radio wavelengths. The exasperated Huth then sped across the flight path of Fink's formation, dodging his Messerschmitt this way and that, trying to signal Fink and the others to turn back. Fink was puzzled at Huth's antics but kept on course. Clouds then hid the fighters and the bombers from each other, and when Fink's Do 17s broke into the clear the 110s had vanished.

Fink's bombers swept across Eastchurch at 1,500 feet and loosed their bombs, destroying hangars, cratering runways and blasting five aircraft. But the planes were not the intended fighters; they were Blenheim bombers. The frequently slipshod Luftwaffe intelligence organization had pinpointed Eastchurch as a Fighter Command base when in fact it belonged to Coastal Command; no Spitfires or Hurricanes were stationed there.

Worse fortune followed. Fink's formation, now ragged after the attack and the ensuing flight through broken cloud cover, was lashed by British fighters. Five bombers were destroyed, and five more landed in France too riddled to take to the air again. Fink climbed out of his seat in a fury and called Kesselring to complain about the incredible confusion. Kesselring left his underground headquarters at Cap Blanc-Nez, near Calais, and journeyed to Arras to offer personal apologies for the mix-up to the apoplectic Fink.

Fink's misadventure was a portent of things to come later that day. A flight of about 30 Ju 88s was grounded because of the postponement order, but word did not reach the bombers' fighter escort of 23 Me 110s. The fighter pilots flew to the intended target at Portland, where Hurricanes shot down six of them. Later in the afternoon, 40 Stukas and a like number of 110s were bounced by 13 Spitfires over Lyme Bay. At the height of the battle, RAF Pilot Officer David Crook looked down to see five Stukas plummeting to earth in flames "more or less in formation."

Then, at five that afternoon, 52 Ju 87s from Richthofen's famous Fliegerkorps VIII, along with an escort of Me 109s, flew over the Salisbury Plain and tried to locate airfields hidden beneath the heavy clouds that still clung to Britain's south coast. They gave up the search and flew back across the Channel, bringing their bombs home with them. Richthofen was the first to admit his attack "was a flop."

Not until the close of Eagle Day, shortly after 5 p.m., did the Luftwaffe execute a perfect attack. An entire *Geschwader* of some 100 Me 109s swept ahead of 86 Ju 87s to engage Spitfires over the field at Detling, near Maidstone. The Stukas, led by Captain Berndt von Brauchitsch, attacked Detling unopposed. Workshops, mess halls and the operations office were blown to pieces, and 22 British planes were destroyed on the ground. Then the Me 109s dropped down through the rising smoke and crisscrossed the field at treetop level, firing cannon and machine guns. Sixty-seven of the staff at Detling, including the station commander, were killed. But Detling, like the field that Fink had assaulted at East-

Clouds of smoke rise from the British airfield at Kenley after a Luftwaffe bomber raid. In two weeks of strikes against RAF airfields between August 24 and September 6, more than 460 Hurricanes and Spitfires were either damaged or destroyed.

church, was a Coastal Command base and housed no fighter planes.

Twelve hours of confused and almost continuous battle produced fantastic claims from both sides. The RAF took credit for 78 German planes destroyed and another 33 probables; the Luftwaffe actually lost only 46. Jubilant Luftwaffe pilots said that they had downed 88 British fighters; in fact, just 13 Spitfires and Hurricanes were shot down, while 47 trainers, bombers and reconnaissance planes were destroyed on the ground. The Luftwaffe report further claimed "eight major airfields virtually destroyed," when in fact not one Fighter Command base was put out of action. Now the German High Command geared up for another major assault on the 15th, and from his command post at Karinhall, Göring ordered Hans-Jürgen Stumpff's Luftflotte 5 to the battle.

Stumpff's squadrons were scattered across occupied Norway and Denmark, where the late-summer weather is usually foul. On the day of the attack it was raining and overcast from Stavanger, Norway, all the way south to Brittany, and the fliers of Luftflotte 5 were sure that there could be no strike against England that day. But by midmorning the clouds had blown away and a blue sky beckoned. The attack was on.

Stumpff planned a double assault, one from Norway, one from Denmark. To fool the British, he sent a decoy flight of 20 He 115 seaplanes toward Scotland to be picked up by radar and so draw RAF fighters far to the north of where 73 of his Heinkel bombers would make landfall. The ruse worked just as Stumpff had intended; RAF fighters rose to attack the seaplanes. But then the bombers and their 21 Me 110 escorts made a navigation error that put them in the same airspace as the decoys; a dozen Spitfires struck from out of the sun, downing 15 German planes. After releasing their bombs, some of the attackers managed to fight their way to the coast.

Stumpff's Ju 88s, attacking from Aalborg, Denmark, flew without escort, depending on speed and their own defensive guns to get them to the target and back. The 50 planes fought their way through to bomb Driffield, north of the port city of Hull, where 10 Whitley bombers were destroyed on the ground, but they were savaged by Spitfires and Hurricanes in a running battle that saw seven Ju 88s shot out of the sky; three others were damaged and crash-landed at far-flung spots along the European coast.

Farther south, Sperrle and Kesselring struck against southeast England throughout the long afternoon and evening of the 15th. Among the Luftwaffe units thrown into action against the RAF that day was Walter Rubensdörffer's Experimental Group 210, which streaked over a Hurricane base at Martlesham Heath, near Ipswich, and left behind a cratered runway and blazing hangars, maintenance facilities and supplies. Rubensdörffer and his pilots then hurried for their home base, where they refueled and rearmed.

At 7:35 p.m. the group crossed the British coastline once more, this time bound for an important RAF base at Kenley, to the south of London. Hoping to catch the British off guard by approaching his target from an unexpected direction, Rubensdörffer decided to lead his strike force in a wide arc around the target and strike Kenley from the north. But faulty navigation led him not to Kenley but to London's Croydon airfield, where the Experimental Group destroyed hangars and 36 training planes. Its bombs also struck nearby houses, killing 62 civilians.

Following this attack, two Hurricane squadrons pounced on the Luftwaffe planes. Outnumbered, the German pilots fought for altitude and went into a tight defensive circle; not long afterward, Rubensdörffer saw a clear patch of sky and broke for home, trailed by four of his Me 110s. "They disappeared into the mist," said the unit's report on the action over Croydon, "and were not seen again."

The other planes of the Experimental Group fought their way home. But the loss of Rubensdörffer and the four pilots who followed him— probably shot down by aggressive Spitfires—helped to bring the Luftwaffe's total losses for that day to 75 bombers and fighters. By contrast, the RAF's vital fighter strength had been reduced by just 34 Spitfires and Hurricanes. The Luftwaffe came out better the next day, losing 38 planes while destroying 50 British aircraft. Then on August 18 the Luftwaffe lost 71 of its planes, including nearly 30 Stuka dive bombers. In return, the German attackers inflicted severe damage on several RAF bases and radar stations but managed to destroy only 17 British fighters.

The following day, Göring once more summoned his top commanders to Karinhall. He made no bones about being displeased with their progress in the air battle against Britain. Yet another new strategy was in order, he said. Attacks on coastal radar stations were a waste of time, according to Göring, and would cease immediately. Air strikes would now be directed farther inland, concentrating on the Fighter Command sector airfields ringing London, fields from which the RAF's Spitfires and Hurricanes were guided into combat by radio. And the Me 109s

Standing on the ventral-hatch ladder of an He 59 floatplane, a rescue crewman hoists aboard the lifeless body of a Luftwaffe flier. German efforts to save airmen downed at sea included search patrols and a network of life rafts anchored in the English Channel.

would no longer be permitted to range freely over Britain in pursuit of their quarry; their mission now was to fly close support for Luftwaffe bomber formations as they assaulted British bases.

Kesselring's airmen in Luftflotte 2 would play the leading role in the new assault—they were much closer to London than were Sperrle's squadrons in Luftflotte 3—and all of Sperrle's Me 109s were transferred to the Pas-de-Calais area to operate with Luftflotte 2.

In the weeks that followed, Kesselring pressed home the attacks Göring had ordered on Fighter Command's vital sector stations ringing London—Biggin Hill, Kenley, Northolt, Duxford, Debden, North Weald, Hornchurch—flying as many as 1,700 sorties a day. For the Me 109 pilots, it was an especially grueling business. Their planes were severely limited by an operating radius of only about 100 miles, and after flying to the vicinity of London they had enough fuel, at most, for only 20 minutes of combat before having to turn for France. A great many of them failed to make it. Lieutenant Hellmuth Ostermann recalled how he and 11 other Me 109 pilots headed back across the Channel with the fuel-warning lights blazing red in every cockpit. One after another, seven planes had to drop down and ditch in the choppy waters. Ostermann and four others landed with dead engines on the French beach.

In spite of such problems, Kesselring's tactics were beginning to work. More Spitfires and Hurricanes were now being destroyed than could be replaced, and 231 of Dowding's more experienced pilots were dead, missing or hospitalized. Their places were taken by Bomber, Coastal and Training Command pilots who were rushed through a few hours of transition training and sent into combat. Six of the vital sector airfields were badly damaged, barely able to scramble enough fighters to intercept the large formations Kesselring was now sending at them from every direction. Fighter Command was reeling, awaiting the knockout punch.

On September 3, while 30 Do 17s were bombing the sector station at North Weald, north of London, with crippling effect, Göring, Sperrle and Kesselring again gathered, this time at The Hague, in an attempt to bring the battle to a quick end. Göring was armed with the latest intelligence report, which claimed that 1,115 British fighters had been destroyed since August 8. The ebullient Kesselring believed the figure, telling Göring that he doubted if the RAF had 100 fighters to commit. The hardheaded Sperrle, whose formations were still being chopped up while crossing the Channel, placed no credence in the report and said he believed Fighter Command could put about 1,000 Spitfires and Hurricanes in the air. In fact, Fighter Command had 621 fighters operational that day.

Göring, ever the optimist, sided with Kesselring and determined that London itself would now feel the Luftwaffe's fury. This, he believed, would draw the last remnants of Fighter Command into the air, to be quickly dispatched. Such a plan was well suited to Hitler's

Manned by a crew of five, the Condor was armed with six guns and carried four 551-pound bombs to use on ships at sea.

An airliner that went to war

Called the "scourge of the Atlantic" by Winston Churchill, the Focke-Wulf 200 Condor was a masterpiece of improvisation. Built as a commercial airliner that could fly nonstop from Berlin to New York, the Condor had greater range than any of the Luftwaffe's bombers. German planners had a fleet of Condors armed and sent them off to prey on the merchant ships that were keeping Great Britain alive after Dunkirk.

Because the merchant convoys were weakly defended, the planes were successful for a time. Flying marathon patrols from the coast of France to occupied Norway and working in concert with U-boats, they made the North Atlantic a hazardous place for Allied shipping. Between August 1940 and February 1941, the Condors of one unit sank 85 Allied vessels totaling 363,000 tons.

But the plane was not strong enough for the rigors of daily combat. More than one Condor broke in half while landing. And when the British bolstered the defense of their shipping lanes with regular fighter patrols, the Condor's lack of armor made it an all too easy mark. In 1944 the plane was unceremoniously returned to the prosaic role of a transport.

A near miss from a Condor sends water flying above the liner Windsor Castle. Condor pilots often made bombing runs barely higher than the masts of the ships they were attacking.

The score card that decorates the tail of this veteran Focke-Wulf 200 records 10 merchant vessels sunk near Narvik, Norway, and 17 sunk off the coast of England.

new turn of mind. During a night raid on August 24-25 an He 111 had overshot its assigned target, oil storage tanks about 20 miles to the east of London, and accidentally unloaded its bombs near the center of the capital. Damage and casualties were light, but Churchill had ordered reprisal raids on Berlin.

Speaking in Berlin on September 4, Hitler threatened to retaliate by razing British cities. "We will stop the handiwork of these air pirates," he said, "so help us God." The day before, the Führer had set a new date for the invasion of England: September 20. Time was running out for Hermann Göring and his Luftwaffe.

Shortly before 4 p.m. on September 7, Göring and Kesselring stood together at Cap Blanc-Nez on the French coast. To the German news correspondents who had been invited to accompany them, Göring declared: "I have taken over personal command of the Luftwaffe in its war against England." Almost as he spoke, the first of some 625 German bombers, supported by about 650 fighter planes, arrowed overhead on their way across the Channel toward London.

Flying in tight formation, the leading wave of attackers reached its targets by 5 p.m. and began raining bombs on the Royal Arsenal near Woolwich. Subsequent German formations, their fighter escorts fending off the sparse squadrons of Spitfires and Hurricanes that rose to meet them, roared through heavy antiaircraft fire to strike at the docks in East London. Huge clouds of smoke billowed over the city, and a Hurricane pilot who flew overhead noted that the "whole eastern suburb of London seemed to be burning."

The raiders turned for home, and for a time the skies were quiet. Then at dusk the bombers returned, guided to their targets by the blazing city. For seven hours the Luftwaffe pounded London with high explosives and incendiaries, and as dawn broke the city lay under a black pall of smoke. Below, nearly 450 Londoners were dead and more than 1,000 were injured. But the Luftwaffe had paid a stiff price, too: The English countryside was littered with the wreckage of 41 German bombers.

The cost to the Luftwaffe would be higher as the assault on London continued day after day. For by concentrating now on the British capital, the Germans left unmolested the RAF's fighter bases, and the skies over Britain were soon swarming with Spitfires and Hurricanes. On September 15, the day of the most concentrated attack, a returning bomber crew reported: "Over the target we were met by enemy fighter formations of up to 80 aircraft." At one point during the action, some 300 RAF fighters were aloft at the same time.

The British pilots did deadly work that day, though German airmen tried valiantly to complete their missions. One Do 17 was hit by enemy fire as it wheeled in a wide circle over London after dropping its load of high explosives. The bomber's crew saw a bright flash, and then black smoke and icy wind poured through the Dornier. "The cabin was full of blood," radio operator Horst Zander would recall later. "Our pilot was hit.'' Through his earphones, Zander heard the stricken pilot talking to his observer, a novice flier. "You have to fly us home," the pilot rasped.

By now the Do 17 was staggering over the North Sea. Zander broke radio silence to request a navigational bearing from a Luftwaffe base in Belgium, and the observer took over the controls. Twenty minutes later, the plane limped safely in to its home field.

Fifty-six Luftwaffe planes were lost, among them 24 Do 17s and 10 He 111s. Counting the many that were severely damaged, fully 25 per cent of the bomber force had been knocked out of action. It was apparent that Britain's Fighter Command, on the other hand, was now stronger than ever.

On September 17, Hitler postponed Operation *Sea Lion* indefinitely. The invasion plan would not be resurrected.

Even so, Göring continued his aerial bombardment of London and other British cities, hoping that England might be brought to its knees by air power alone. In early October, however, he realized that his Luftwaffe could no longer sustain the mounting losses inflicted during daylight raids by a resurgent Fighter Command. Henceforth, he decreed, German bombers would attack under cover of darkness.

He could not have picked a worse time of year to begin night flying. With the approach of winter, the weather was deteriorating. Day after day, the bombers took off at dusk from their fields in France and northern Belgium, wheels lifting from sodden runways, light rain whipping against the windshields. More often than not the planes had to fly through heavy clouds to reach their assigned altitudes for the approach to London, and these crews of the autumn were not the veterans of the summer. Many of the most seasoned of the Luftwaffe's all-weather fliers were either dead or in British prisoner-of-war camps after crash-landing or parachuting in enemy territory. Inexperienced German pilots and navigators had great difficulty in hitting the rendezvous point on time, and there was much dangerous milling around in the dark sky before the bombers could form up and set course for London.

Despite these operational difficulties, Sperrle's and Kesselring's bomber crews began the nighttime blitz. When the weather was marginal an average of 160 bombers managed to reach London to unload some 200 tons of high explosive and thousands of incendiaries. On October 15, when there was a full moon, the Luftwaffe managed to get 410 bombers over London to unload nearly 600 tons of bombs. Docks blazed, whole blocks were churned to rubble and 1,300 Britons were killed or wounded.

The night bombers struck as far north as Glasgow, in Scotland, and as far south as Portsmouth. The most famous of all the nighttime blitz raids occurred on November 14, when 449 German bombers, guided by a radio signal beamed from the French coast, unloaded 500 tons of high explosive and 30 tons of incendiaries on Coventry. More than 100 acres of the city's center were gutted; the medieval cathedral was reduced to a burned-out shell and one third of Coventry's homes were smashed.

Adolf Galland, who tallied 57 kills to become Germany's top air ace in the Battle of Britain, climbs down from an Me 109 sporting a cigar-smoking Mickey Mouse.

Although his 55 kills put him third among Luftwaffe pilots in the Battle of Britain, Werner Mölders later became the first German pilot to pass the 100-kill mark.

Helmut Wick reenacts for his comrades one of the 56 kills that made him the Luftwaffe's second-ranking fighter pilot in the air war against Britain.

One of the German bomber pilots later wrote: "The usual cheers that greeted a direct hit stuck in our throats. The crew just gazed down on the sea of flames in silence. Was this really a military target?"

Indeed, Coventry was. Of the 21 factories that were hit within the city, 12 were heavily involved in production of aircraft components.

After Coventry, the attacks tapered off considerably during the foul-weather nights of winter but picked up again in the early spring as the Luftwaffe hurled growing numbers of bombers against the British. Then on May 10, 1941, in one of the War's heaviest assaults against the British capital, more than 500 bombers thundered over London and dropped some 700 tons of high explosive and incendiaries.

Luftwaffe airmen, assured by their commanders that they were delivering the crushing blow against an already reeling Britain, were charged with excitement as they set out on their missions that night. Some of them, like the combat-seasoned Captain Albert Hufenreuter, worried about the RAF night fighters that were sure to greet them in the skies over London, but they drew solace from their belief that the vast formations of raiders would confuse and overtax the British defenders.

It was indeed a historic assault—but for a different reason. For in the wake of this attack, even the most optimistic Luftwaffe leaders would come to the full realization that they were no nearer to bringing Britain to its knees through aerial attack than they had been the previous summer.

The 25-year-old Hufenreuter, the airplane commander, was lying on his stomach in the navigator-bombardier's position in his Heinkel 111

Seen from a Dornier 17, London burns under Luftwaffe attack. Between September and November 1940, bombings killed 13,000 Londoners.

as the plane took off at 10:30 p.m. from its French base near Lille. Soon he could see the whitecaps of the Channel, 12,000 feet below. When the bomber neared the British coast, Hufenreuter spoke on his intercom to his pilot, Sergeant Richard Furthmann. Hufenreuter directed Furthmann to fly a zigzag course to the target. Long before reaching London he could see the glow of fires left behind by preceding waves of bombers. He could also see the British searchlights knifing skyward.

The bomber was getting closer to the target area now, and Hufenreuter could plainly make out the moonlit serpentine course of the Thames that had become so familiar to Luftwaffe bomber crews. He gave more directions to Furthmann and then told him: "We're right dead on track and the target should be coming up any minute."

Hufenreuter dropped his 1,000-pound high-explosive bomb from 9,000 feet at a few minutes after midnight. But his work was not over. "Keep her on the river," he commanded the pilot. "We'll see what the incendiaries will do." As Furthmann steered the Heinkel over the Thames, it was easy to see what the earlier raiders' incendiaries had done. The whole river shore seemed to be a mass of darting flames, flames that would serve as targets for still more formations of Luftwaffe bombers. Hufenreuter dropped his four canisters of incendiaries on the center of the city and then set a course for home. Hufenreuter's He 111 and its companion planes had done their best to deliver a knockout blow; would it be enough?

As the Heinkel turned south, Hufenreuter warned the crewmen to keep a sharp watch for British night fighters. Suddenly he saw ominous streams of tracer bullets slicing around the bomber's left engine. Furthmann shoved the plane into a dive, trying to escape his pursuer. At that moment the engine went dead, its propeller spinning out of control. Diving still lower, Furthmann shook the British fighter, but the badly damaged Heinkel could not make it back to France.

The pilot tried to keep the plane aloft, but it was losing altitude fast. It was down to 1,000 feet, then even lower. Finally, Furthmann shouted: "Captain, I can't hold her!" The Heinkel pancaked onto a farm field near Ashford, Kent, and slammed to a stop against a windbreak of sturdy hawthorn trees. All the crew members were injured in the crash, and all became prisoners of war.

Hufenreuter's Heinkel was one of only 14 German bombers lost in the massive raid, which killed nearly 1,500 Londoners and destroyed some 700 acres of the city by fire. But the British, as they had done after previous raids, put out the fires, began clearing the rubble and braced for the next assault. By June the air attacks had ebbed and then trickled away. Now, it was evident that further assaults would bring Britain little closer to defeat. The Luftwaffe's thrusts against England had been blunted, and the Battle of Britain was over. In the final tally, the RAF had lost some 1,000 aircraft in repelling the German raiders; Luftwaffe losses stood at about 2,000 planes. And German airmen still had other enemies to face, and many more air battles ahead. ～

The Battle of Britain through German eyes

Having once dreamed of becoming a painter (a dream thwarted when he was twice denied admission to art school because of insufficient talent), Adolf Hitler considered himself an authority on aesthetic matters. When the Führer learned in 1941 that a few of his generals had appointed amateur artists to record military exploits on canvas, he called a halt to the practice and ordered the German High Command to recruit professional painters who could document the feats of the Reich's armed forces in properly heroic style. From this edict, a new military department, the *Kriegsmaler und Pressezeichner* (War Painters and Press Artists), was born. By 1942, the organization had grown from 45 artists to 80 and had acquired a pretentious new name—*Staffel der Bildenden Künstler,* or Squadron of Pictorial Artists.

Those artists who were assigned to the Luftwaffe soon found themselves in the thick of the fighting. Sent aloft on bombing missions, they struggled to sketch the action while the planes careened through the air, dodging antiaircraft fire and machine-gun bursts from enemy fighters. When they were unable to go along, as on fighter attacks with one-man planes, they relied for detail on pilots' debriefing reports and mission photographs. After serving three months in the field, each artist was permitted to retreat to a studio back home, where he spent the next three months transforming his sketches into full-blown oil paintings or watercolors. A sampling from the work of two Luftwaffe artists appears here and on the following pages.

The propaganda value of the government-sponsored artworks was exploited to the utmost. Widely exhibited in German museums, reproduced in magazines and even replicated on picture postcards, these visions of aerial glory boosted the morale of airmen and civilians alike. The paintings were also transported to museums in German-controlled nations throughout Europe, where they served as graphic reminders of the Luftwaffe's might.

Closing in for attack from astern, Messerschmitt 109s (foreground) intercept a formation of Royal Air Force bombers approaching the coast of occupied France.

Stukas brave antiaircraft fire from a shoreside gun to dive-bomb merchant vessels in a British harbor.

While an RAF air crew bails out of a plunging Sunderland flying boat, an Me 109 streaks away to find another victim.

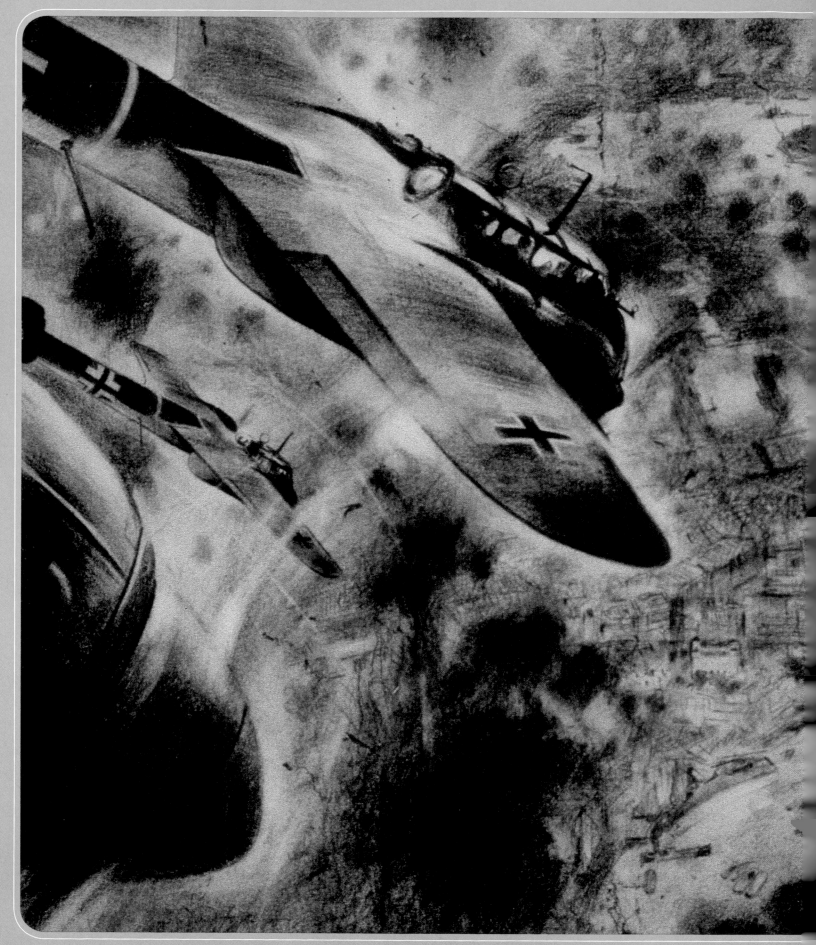

Angling in toward London's Tower Bridge, Domier 17 bombers prepare to attack the docks and warehouses along the Thames River.

4

The Luftwaffe spread thin

In the spring of 1941, when it was becoming clear that the Luftwaffe could not, with its present force, batter the stubborn British into submission, Reich Marshal Hermann Göring arrived in occupied Paris and summoned all of his air commanders stationed in France. Göring brought, he said, electrifying news: The Luftwaffe formations along the English Channel would be heavily reinforced, the attacks on England would be resumed with new fury and England would be invaded.

This was a surprising announcement, since Hitler and Göring appeared to have given up hope of conquering Britain. After dropping this bombshell, Göring pulled aside his two most brilliant fighter pilots and air commanders, Werner Mölders and Adolf Galland. "He chuckled softly and rubbed his hands with glee," Galland later wrote. The entire speech, Göring confided, had been part of an elaborate smoke screen designed to hide, even from his own Luftwaffe fliers, the Führer's true intention, which was "the imminent invasion of the Soviet Union."

This news came as "a paralyzing shock," Galland remembered. "The dread that had been hanging over us like the sword of Damocles since the beginning of the War would now become a reality: war on two fronts. I could think of nothing else but the dark and sinister vision of starting a war with the Soviet Union, so tremendously strong in manpower and natural resources, while our strength had already proved insufficient to conquer the British in the first assault. Now we were to turn against a new, unknown, and in any case gigantic, enemy, without having first cleared our rear."

Göring reassured Galland that Stalin's Russia was so rotten internally that it would crumble at the first blow. As for the Soviet Air Force, "it would only be necessary to shoot down the leader of a flight for the remaining illiterates to lose themselves on the way home." Then they could be knocked off "like clay pigeons."

The fighter ace was not convinced. He left still fearing for the Luftwaffe's—and Germany's—future. The reality would exceed Galland's apprehensions as the Luftwaffe and the rest of the armed forces

The front cargo doors of a huge Messerschmitt Gigant open to load horses. The six-engined transport, which could carry 25,000 pounds of freight, became a vital cargo carrier on the vast Eastern Front after Hitler's invasion of the Soviet Union.

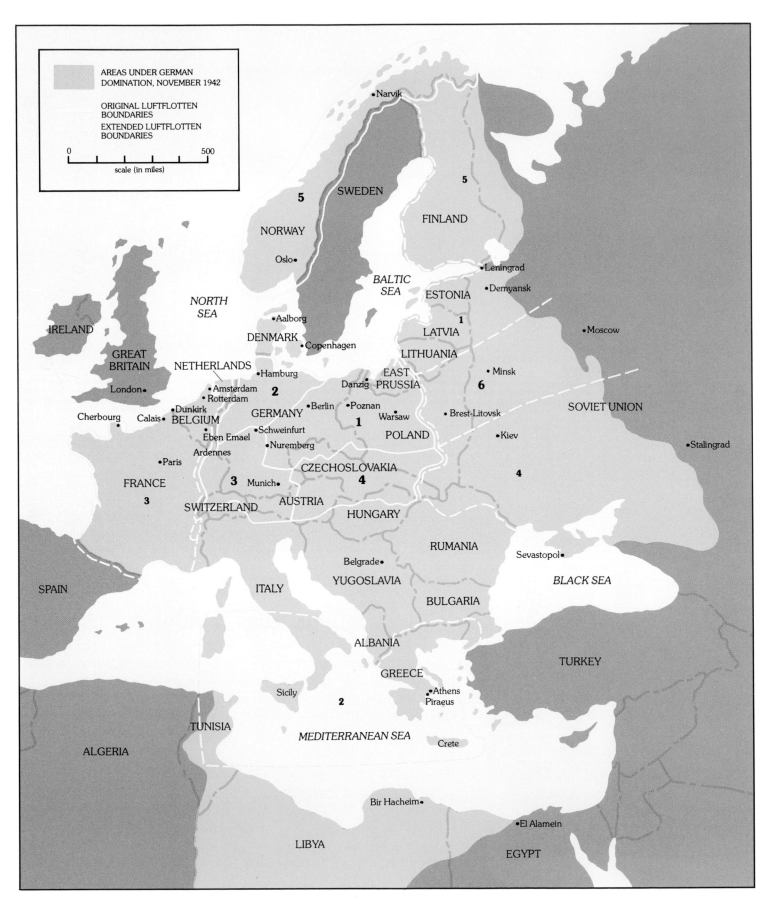

found themselves not only locked in an enormous conflict with the Soviet Union but also fighting on a third front in the Mediterranean.

Hitler's decision to attack Russia was based less on military realities than on the Führer's grandiose vision of Germany's historical destiny. It was, Hitler believed, the ordained mission of the "superior" Nordic Germans to conquer and rule the Slavic peoples, gaining *Lebensraum* and eradicating Bolshevism in the process.

The invasion of Russia—code-named Operation *Barbarossa* and originally scheduled for May 1941—was an undertaking so Gargantuan that it staggered General Guderian and other hardheaded Army commanders. Three million men in 148 divisions, supported by 3,300 tanks and 2,000 serviceable Luftwaffe bombers and fighters, would be required to launch the attack along a frontier stretching 1,000 miles from East Prussia in the north to the Black Sea in the south.

Before the Russian campaign could start, however, Hitler was forced to shore up his Balkan flank, where his ally Mussolini had run into trouble. In October 1940, Italian forces had invaded Greece, moving southward from Albania, which was already in Il Duce's hands. But the Italian troops were soon retreating before the tough Greek infantry. To help the Greeks defend their homeland, Britain sent a 50,000-man expeditionary force ashore near Athens in March 1941, having already occupied the Greek island of Crete. From the German point of view this posed a threat of the first order: British bombers stationed on Crete would be within range of Rumania, Germany's ally, whose oil fields were essential to the war effort.

The Luftwaffe, it developed, was already poised for a counterstroke. It had more than 400 warplanes based on Rumanian fields, where German work crews had labored through the winter building barracks, hangars and repair shops. When in March 1941 friendly Bulgaria permitted German forces to be stationed there, 120 Luftwaffe bombers, fighters and reconnaissance planes were flown south to bring them that much closer to Greece.

This aerial armada belonged to Luftflotte 4, commanded by General Alexander Löhr, who had used tactical air power with such telling effect during the blitzkrieg on Poland. Löhr, busy with plans for the Russian invasion, enlisted his old colleague, General Wolfram von Richthofen, in running day-to-day air operations in the Balkans. When on March 27 Yugoslavia, which had seemed to be ready to fall into the Axis camp, was convulsed by an anti-German coup d'état, another target was added to Richthofen's list. The Führer ordered simultaneous attacks on Greece and Yugoslavia to begin on the morning of April 6.

Dawn broke fair and clear over the Balkans as squadrons of He 111s, Ju 88s, Ju 87s, Me 109s and Me 110s lifted from eight separate airfields. Some headed westward toward Belgrade, Yugoslavia's capital, some south toward Greece. The savage raid on Belgrade, and two more on the following days by both Stukas and three *Gruppen* of twin-engined medium bombers, flattened much of the city and killed, by some esti-

Germany's widespread conquests— mapped here at the 1942 peak (shaded area)—required an extension of the Luftwaffe's original four Luftflotten, or air fleets, well beyond their original boundaries (solid yellow lines). Not only was each expanded (broken yellow lines) but two new Luftflotten were added, one in Norway, the other in the Soviet Union.

mates, 17,000 people. Hammered without respite from the sky, their capital in ruins, Yugoslav ground forces collapsed within a week. By April 13, German victory flags were flying over Belgrade. The cost: 558 German lives and a handful of airplanes.

The Luftwaffe planes that had gone on to Greece bombed the Greek and British frontline positions, preparing the way for Field Marshal Wilhelm List's Twelfth Army, and also attacked rear-area supply facilities. One Gruppe of Ju 88s bored in on Piraeus, the port just to the south of Athens, to destroy the docks and lay mines in the harbor. Captain Hajo Herrmann, one of the Luftwaffe's most skilled bomber pilots, took his Ju 88 down to about 500 feet and zeroed in on an innocent-looking freighter that was tied up at the quay. The ship was the *Clan Frazer* and she was loaded with 250 tons of high explosive. Herrmann's 500-pound bomb dropped directly onto the Scottish vessel. The explosion was cataclysmic: The *Clan Frazer* disappeared, taking 12 other ships with her, and the port was unusable for weeks to come. Herrmann and his men had caused more destruction than any other single Luftwaffe bomber crew since the beginning of the War.

Three Dornier 17s streak over Athens' ancient Acropolis shortly after the German conquest of Greece in April 1941. Ceaseless Luftwaffe attacks on the enemy defenses enabled the Twelfth Army's troops to advance from Greece's northern border to the capital in three weeks.

With other Luftwaffe squadrons providing superb cover, List's army poured through the mountain passes of northern Greece, the tank spearheads relentlessly pushing back the combined force of Greek and British infantry. The sky was filled with Richthofen's machine-gunning and bomb-dropping Stukas while the Messerschmitt 109s and 110s handily dealt with the few British retaliatory strikes.

On April 20, more than 100 Ju 88s, heavily escorted by Me 109s and 110s, raided the main British air base in Greece, a large airfield near Piraeus. Fifteen Hurricanes—all that were available—rose to fend off the attackers. In a huge, confused dogfight that spread all over the skies of southern Greece, the RAF fighters downed 14 planes. But the British lost five of their dwindling number of fighters, and the 10 Hurricanes that limped home were badly shot up.

With their aircraft virtually unopposed, the Luftwaffe continued to harry the retreating Greek and British forces. The British high command in London, recognizing that the game was up, ordered the evacuation of what remained of its expeditionary force by sea to Crete. By April 30, the last of the British had withdrawn.

The German victories in Greece and Yugoslavia did not solve all of Hitler's problems. The British still controlled Crete. General Löhr suggested to Hitler that the Luftwaffe's elite parachute troops and glider infantry could remove this thorn in the Germans' side with an airborne assault on the island. Hitler agreed, and so did Göring. Soon General Kurt Student, commander of Germany's airborne divisions, was closeted with the Führer, who declared that the capture of Crete from the air would be the "crowning glory" of his Balkan campaign. The island would give him a base from which to launch aerial attacks on the Suez Canal and the great British naval base at Alexandria. On April 25, Hitler ordered the winged operation set in motion.

Student had less than three weeks to prepare for the assault. Virtually the entire fleet of workhorse Ju 52 transports, used hard during the Balkan fighting to carry ammunition and supplies over the mountainous terrain, had to be flown to maintenance centers in Germany, Austria and Czechoslovakia for overhaul. Within two weeks, 493 of the refurbished Iron Annies were back in Greece ready for combat, but the landing sites assigned them were little more than stretches of sandy ground nestled between hills. When one of the transport commanders, Colonel Rüdiger von Heyking, saw the strips ringing Athens, he protested. "They are nothing but deserts! Heavily laden aircraft will sink up to their axles." In practice takeoffs the transports raised billowing clouds of yellow dust that swirled to 3,000 feet, obscuring the sun and preventing further flights for almost 20 minutes.

While their transports were scattered at maintenance depots throughout the Reich, the airborne regiments in Germany were obliged to go south by rail and aboard trucks. Traffic jams on narrow Balkan roads slowed the truck convoys to a crawl. One entire airborne division, the 22nd, never got farther than a railroad siding outside a remote Rumanian village, and the 5th Mountain Division, already in Greece, had to substitute for them in the assault force at the last minute.

Despite such vexations, Student managed to muster 22,750 combat troops in Greece by May 18. Of these, 750 would be launched in gliders, 10,000 would descend by parachute, 5,000 would land on Crete aboard Ju 52s and 7,000 would go by boat.

To soften up the British, the 180 medium bombers and 132 dive bombers of Richthofen's Fliegerkorps began pounding Crete. The island's 42,000-man garrison consisted of a heterogeneous lot of New Zealanders, Australians and British, most of them recently evacuated from Greece without their weapons, plus a mixed bag of Greek troops and Cretan irregulars armed with fowling pieces and ancient swords. These ill-equipped defenders had little artillery, and even small-arms ammunition was scarce because Richthofen's Stukas were attacking the ships sent to relieve the island. Supplies arriving at the main Cretan port of Suda Bay dropped from 700 tons a day to 100 tons.

Recognizing the extreme gravity of the situation, Churchill put the garrison under the command of Major General Bernard Freyberg, a hardy New Zealander, a veteran of World War I who had been wounded 12 times and had won four Distinguished Service Orders and the Victoria Cross. He set his men to work digging slit trenches and gun emplacements around three airfields spaced about 100 miles apart on the island's northern coast. The main assaults were expected there. Freyberg's forceful, buoyant personality did much to improve morale despite the fact that Luftwaffe planes were constantly overhead.

The Luftwaffe bombers first smashed Crete's harbors; then they pummeled the airfields and antiaircraft guns. The handful of RAF Hurricanes and Gladiators on Crete rose to take on the He 111s and Ju 88s, but they were swamped by the escorting 109s. By May 19 only seven fighters remained. They could do nothing to stem the tide, and so they took off at first light for the safety of Egypt. The skies over the beleaguered island now belonged entirely to the Luftwaffe.

The day set for the German airborne assault, May 20, dawned clear, warm and windless. Squadron after squadron of twin-engined Luftwaffe planes roared off runways in southern Greece and headed across the Aegean. By 6 o'clock they were bombing the village and airfield at Maleme near the western tip of the island, where the first wave of gliderborne infantry and paratroops was scheduled to land. The medium bombers were followed by howling packs of Stukas and by Me 109s and 110s that whipped low over the churned-up earth firing machine guns and cannon and pinning the British and Greek defenders in their slit trenches.

Now overhead came a stately procession of Ju 52s, each towing a deep-bellied, tapered-wing DFS 230 glider carrying 10 troopers of Student's crack assault regiment. The towlines were unhooked and the gliders dipped toward Crete's craggy terrain.

Trouble for the Germans began when most of the glider pilots, their

Men of the 5th Mountain Division, pressed into duty as airborne troopers, wait on a Greek airfield to board Ju 52s for the 150-mile flight to Crete. Landing amid heavy British fire, these tough soldiers helped secure the vital Maleme airfield and pave the way for the German victory.

visibility curtailed by the smoke and dust of the bombardment, overshot their targets. The DFS 230s slammed into the ground far apart from one another. As the troopers scrambled from the smashed gliders, they found themselves isolated in deep ravines, prevented from joining together by fierce fire from the New Zealand defenders.

Behind the gliders streamed formations of Ju 52s laden with parachute infantry. Shells from the British 40-millimeter Bofors antiaircraft guns ripped into some of the transports before the men could jump. A New Zealander watched a Ju 52 breaking apart, "the bodies falling out like potato sacks." The parachutists who managed to hurl themselves through the open doors of the transports immediately came under heavy rifle and machine-gun fire from the defenders below, most of whom had survived the bombing and strafing attacks in their slit trenches. Scores of the Germans floating earthward died in their parachute harnesses. Those who reached the ground alive thudded into terraced vineyards, onto rooftops and into barley fields.

The 3rd Battalion landed in the middle of a fortified New Zealand position and was shot to pieces; within an hour all of its officers were

either dead or wounded. One New Zealand officer remembered the bodies lying in a vineyard, "many still in their harnesses with the parachutes tugging at them in every mild puff of breeze and getting no response. Among the olives corpses hung from branches or lay at the foot of gnarled trees, motionless on the trampled young barley."

The German assault on Canea, a town east of Maleme and the administrative capital of Crete, fared no better. Four of 15 gliders splashed into the sea while the others landed too far apart. Split into small groups, the troops became easy targets, and half were lost before the day was out. Like their comrades at Maleme, the parachutists who followed jumped into a storm of lead. Incendiary bullets set silk canopies ablaze and paratroopers fell screaming in a trail of fire.

The final aerial assault of the day began at 4:15 p.m. with bombing and strafing of the airfields at Rethymnon and Herakleion. The Ju 52s should have been overhead immediately after the last bomb dropped, but all was confusion back on the Greek airfields. The transports that had returned from their morning missions had to be refueled by hand from barrels, and the whirling propellers kicked up such clouds of dust

A Ju 52 transport, hit by British fire, plunges in flames toward a rocky outcrop as paratroops float down near Herakleion airport, a primary German objective during the May 1941 invasion of Crete. More than half of the 493 Ju 52s used in the assault on Crete were lost.

that takeoffs were delayed. The dust became so thick that some of the returning Ju 52s crashed into each other and into fresh transports trying to taxi out. As a result, subsequent assault waves arrived late over Crete and in reduced numbers. The British defenders near Herakleion, who had saved their antiaircraft fire during the earlier bombing, now blasted away. Ten to 15 of the slow transports were shot out of the sky. The men on the ground watched as the planes exploded and the Germans came tumbling out, one eyewitness reported, "like plums from a burst bag. I saw one aircraft flying out to sea with six men trailing from it in the cords of their 'chutes.' "

It was not until evening that the Germans achieved their first, limited measure of success. Near Maleme, Lieutenant Horst Trebes and the regimental surgeon, Dr. Heinrich Neumann, gathered all the glider troops they could find and charged up Hill 107, firing pistols and tossing grenades to take this tactically important site commanding both the town of Maleme and its airfield. They drove the defenders from the crest, then flung themselves down, fearing the British would counterattack. Dr. Neumann remembered that "we were so short of ammunition that, had they done so, we should have had to fight them off with stones and sheath-knives."

Back in Athens Student and Löhr decided to make the most of the seizure of Hill 107. Every reserve the Luftwaffe possessed would be thrown into the battle to capture the airfield; once it was in German hands, elements of the 5th Mountain Division would be flown in to secure the western end of the island.

Early the next morning, five companies of parachute troops descended out of range of British guns and started for Maleme. That afternoon Ju 52s began setting down on the field, which was still under fire. Some of the transports were blown apart by British shells; others slewed crazily when wings were clipped off; still others caught fire. A captured British tank was used to push the wrecks off the field. Other Iron Annies landed, disgorged more troops and lurched back into the air. One of every three transports that flew into Maleme was destroyed or damaged and the perimeter of the field was soon littered with wrecked Ju 52s—80 in all. But by 5 p.m. the field was in German hands.

That night a small flotilla of wooden powerboats seized from Greek fishermen set off for Crete loaded with 2,000 more mountain troops. The boats ran afoul of patrolling British cruisers and destroyers, whose guns sent 3- and 6-inch shells ripping into them. When it was over, the remnants of the flotilla were straggling back for Greece, leaving nearly 300 men dead in the sea.

The Luftwaffe took its revenge on the next two days. Richthofen's He 111s, Do 17s and Ju 88s, and a crack *Geschwader* of some 100 Ju 87s led by veteran Colonel Oskar Dinort, savaged the Royal Navy in an air-sea battle that sent two cruisers and four destroyers to the bottom. Within the next week the Luftwaffe sank four more destroyers and a cruiser and crippled or damaged 13 other British ships.

The rest of the 5th Mountain Division was flown into Maleme to team up with the airborne units and harry the British into the sea. By May 27, General Freyberg had reported to London that his men had reached "the limit of endurance" after "the concentrated bombing that we have been faced with during the last seven days." His conclusion: "Our position here is hopeless."

The Royal Navy began evacuating troops from shattered Herakleion in the early morning hours of May 29. Only 4,000 men were saved; some 3,500 dead and wounded were left behind along with more than 11,000 prisoners. But the Germans had also suffered severely. Luftwaffe casualties totaled 6,116 air crew and airborne troops, nearly 2,000 of whom had been killed. General Student lamented that "Crete was the grave of the German parachutist." Indeed, the Luftwaffe's airborne troops would drop onto a battlefield only once again—in a small and ineffectual operation in late 1944. For the rest of the War they were to be used mainly as regular infantry.

The conquests in the eastern Mediterranean, although swift, had taken longer than Hitler had bargained for, postponing Operation *Barbarossa* from mid-May until June 22. The first strike was launched by the Luftwaffe just as dawn was breaking. Ju 88s and He 111s, flown by specially picked crews, swept across the frontier at designated points from East Prussia to southern Rumania. Their targets: the 66 forward airfields, well scouted by high-altitude Luftwaffe reconnaissance flights, where most of the Soviet Air Force's frontline fighters and bombers were stationed.

This invaluable intelligence had been provided by Colonel Theodor Rowehl, 37, a veteran pilot who had been pioneering photoreconnaissance techniques since 1930. Rowehl's Reconnaissance Group was equipped with swift Dornier 215s, Ju 88s and a handful of older Ju 86s modified for high-altitude flight. Cruising far above the reach of Russian fighters or antiaircraft guns, Rowehl and his crews had been overflying Soviet territory frequently since October 1940, taking thousands of vertical and oblique photographs through long-range Zeiss lenses—in direct defiance of the nonaggression pact Hitler had signed with Stalin in August 1939. Although the Soviet government knew of the flights— two of Rowehl's planes were forced down in Russian territory through mechanical failures—no action was taken, except for formal notes of protest. Stalin's reluctance to remonstrate with his supposed ally thus paved the way for the most crippling air-to-ground strike in history. The German bombers roared across the sleeping countryside and fell upon the Soviet airstrips with thousands of newly developed SD-2 fragmentation bombs. No antiaircraft fire rose from the fields, which were taken completely by surprise. The bombs sent whizzing fragments of metal slicing through the rows of aircraft lined up wing tip to wing tip.

The attacks, timed for 3:15 a.m. to coincide exactly with the opening barrages of artillery fire on the ground, were designed not only to destroy enemy planes but also to demoralize and disrupt the Soviet Air Force so that it would be unable to react to later, larger strikes. Now, with the sun breaking fully across the sky, hundreds of medium bombers, Stukas and fighters roamed freely through Russian airspace, blasting fields, bridges and rail lines. The first strike achieved its purpose. Most of the Soviet planes were still on the ground, where they made easy targets as later waves of Luftwaffe raiders zeroed in on them. The Russian forward airfields were so close to the border that the German airmen were able to fly as many as eight missions on the first day of Operation *Barbarossa*. Their task was made all the easier by the absence of any Soviet advance warning system. By noon the Luftwaffe had destroyed—by the Russians' own count—1,200 Soviet aircraft, two thirds of them on the ground. (The day's total would exceed 2,000.)

A few Russian fighter pilots based on fields farther back managed to get into the air and offer some resistance, but their stubby open-cockpit I.16 fighters—which had been nicknamed *Ratas* (rats) by German Condor Legion pilots during the Spanish Civil War—were hopelessly outclassed by the German fighters.

One Soviet Air Force pilot who rose to do battle on June 22, Lieutenant D. V. Kokorev, initiated the tactic that worked best against the Luftwaffe. When his guns jammed during a dogfight with an Me 110, Kokorev whipped his I.16 around and rammed the 110 head on. Both aircraft slammed into the ground. Zealous—and heedless—Russian pilots used the same tactic often thereafter. Some survived.

As the Wehrmacht's tanks and infantry plunged into Russia, Soviet bomber pilots as well resorted to suicidal methods of trying to halt the advance. Unescorted, they flew outdated twin-engined Tupolev SB bombers in dense formations of up to 60 planes in an effort to disrupt German river crossings. Entire squadrons were blown out of the sky either by Luftwaffe flak gunners, who could hardly miss, or by Me 109s and 110s that chopped the unwieldy formations to pieces.

Russian attempts to retaliate against the Luftwaffe's own airfields were a failure. Captain Herbert Pabst, a Stuka pilot who had just landed after a mission, watched fascinated as a trio of Me 109s tore into a squadron of Russian bombers headed for his field. "When the first one fired," he recalled later, "thin threads of smoke seemed to join it to the bomber. Turning ponderously to the side, the big bird flashed silver, then plunged vertically downward with its engines screaming. As it crashed a huge sheet of flame shot upward. The second bomber became a glare of red, exploded as it dived, and only the bits came floating down like great autumn leaves. The third turned over backward on fire. A similar fate befell the rest." The Russians kept on coming for the rest of the day; "not one got away."

On June 29 the German High Command proudly announced that 4,017 Russian planes had been destroyed at a cost of only 150 Luftwaffe aircraft, figures the Russians did not dispute. With the Soviet Air Force reeling from its catastrophic losses, the three Luftflotten along

the immense front could now throw their full weight behind the tanks and infantry. When General Guderian's Second Panzer Group was brought up short at Brest-Litovsk, Stukas were called in to blast the city's heavily fortified citadel into submission. For an entire day the air was filled with the scream of Ju 87 engines as the planes swooped down to hurl 550-pound bombs on the defenders. But when the dust settled, Brest-Litovsk still held. A special unit of Ju 88s then entered the contest and unloaded 3,500-pound blockbusters that crumpled the citadel's walls. The fortress surrendered the following morning.

Profiting from the excellent air support, the panzers after only one week of fighting had smashed through the first line of Soviet defenses, penetrated 200 miles into Russia on the Central Front, and were moving on the key cities of Kiev in the south, Smolensk in the center and Leningrad in the north. By mid-July, the panzers on the Central Front had advanced 400 miles and were only 200 miles from Moscow.

To keep the Red Army from regrouping, the Luftwaffe—as it had in Poland and France—attacked the railroad system. Groups and squadrons of bombers, and even lone fighter-bombers, winged off each dawn to bomb the all-important Soviet rail line west of the Dnieper River. Holding their fire on locomotives and rolling stock—which the Wehrmacht planned to use later to haul its own supplies—the pilots and bombardiers concentrated on the tracks. Within five days nothing moved along miles of twisted metal and splintered ties, and the Soviet Sixth Army defending the Dnieper was stranded for lack of supplies.

A Stuka wings in low over a pair of German tanks in Russia during the summer of 1941, ready to bomb or strafe any Soviet troops hidden in the distant woods. More than 300 of the deadly Ju 87 dive bombers gave the German ground forces close air support when the Wehrmacht lunged into Russia in June 1941.

The ceaseless attacks on Soviet communications made it impossible for the Russians to mount any major counterattack, and the panzers continued to roll. Between early July and mid-October the Wehrmacht fought seven major battles of encirclement at Minsk, Smolensk, Uman, Gomel and Kiev, along the Sea of Azov, and at Vyazma—the last only 125 miles west of Moscow. Panzer divisions would flank a city, ring it and begin blasting it with artillery. Then the Luftwaffe would jump in, its bombers and fighters hitting everything that moved. Stukas plunged again and again to drop 550- and 110-pound bombs into the masses of infantry, tanks, guns and trucks or to rip apart the divisions advancing in the open to relieve one or another of the cities. When the last of the great encirclements was over, the Germans had captured a staggering 2,256,000 prisoners, 9,336 tanks and 16,170 pieces of artillery.

During the summer of 1941, Luftwaffe fighter pilots, many of whom were to run up fantastic kill totals on the Eastern Front, continued to fatten their scores. A wave of Soviet bombers intent on stopping Guderian's tanks outside Minsk on June 30 ran afoul of Jagdgeschwader 51, led by the German ace Werner Mölders. In the ensuing turkey shoot the 109s knocked 114 of the Russian planes out of the sky, giving Mölders' group the distinction of being the first to destroy 1,000 enemy aircraft. Mölders shot down five planes that day, bringing his personal tally to 82, and two other high-scoring pilots, Hermann-Friedrich Joppien and Heinz Bär, downed five apiece.

The Luftwaffe's huge success in Russia as a ground-support air force masked for a time its fatal flaw: the lack of big, four-engined bombers capable of a sustained offensive against Soviet defense industries. After the invasion, the Russians, with enormous effort, had moved many of their steel mills and tank and aircraft factories beyond the Ural Moun-

A Soviet supply train burns after being attacked by bombers in a photograph taken from a Heinkel 111. In the first six months of the Russian campaign the Luftwaffe flew 6,000 sorties against the enemy rail system; the target was usually tracks rather than rolling stock, which the Germans hoped to save and use.

tains and the reach of the Luftwaffe's medium-range twin-engined bombers. While the German forces were capturing or destroying thousands of Russian planes and tanks, the relocated Soviet industries were pouring out replacements. The Luftwaffe's inability to destroy the Soviet Union's weapons at their source would ultimately lead to catastrophe for Germany's entire war effort.

The Luftwaffe's lack of strategic punch was quickly revealed when, in midsummer 1941, Hitler ordered Moscow "razed to the ground." For the initial raid on the night of July 22, Luftwaffe units on the Central Front could scrape together only 195 Ju 88s and He 111s from six different bomber wings; Russian antiaircraft fire and the wear and tear of ceaseless ground-support missions had taken their toll. As the bombers approached Moscow, the sky lighted up with the blue-white flash of more than 300 searchlights, followed by a blizzard of antiaircraft fire. The bombers disgorged 104 tons of high explosives, and incendiaries by the thousands, but the formations were so disrupted by the bursting antiaircraft shells and blinding searchlights that the bombs were scattered ineffectually across the city.

This first air assault against the heart of the Soviet Union was the largest, and those that came afterward achieved no greater results. In Russia the Luftwaffe was under the operational control of the Army, whose demands for close support of ground operations grew with every yard the tanks and troops advanced. By the end of the year the Luftwaffe was sending only three to 10 bombers to Moscow each night; they did little more than rob the Muscovites of sleep—and a great opportunity to cripple the Soviet defensive effort was lost.

One of the most desperate tasks facing the Luftwaffe in the late summer of 1941 was the neutralization of the Soviet Baltic Fleet. The Wehrmacht had successfully cut off Leningrad from the rest of Russia, but its siege forces had come under murderous fire from Soviet ships stationed at the nearby Kronstadt naval base. Thousands of tons of high-explosive shells landed among the dug-in German infantry and field guns on Leningrad's periphery. The Luftwaffe's job was to sink or disable two Soviet battleships, two cruisers, 27 destroyers and some 200 auxiliary ships. Not only could the ships throw up murderous amounts of antiaircraft fire, but the Kronstadt area itself was packed with heavy and light guns of every caliber, about 600 in all.

Luftwaffe General Helmut Förster first tried high-altitude bombing, sending wave after wave of Ju 88s and He 111s over Kronstadt, but none of the targets were knocked out. It fell to the Stuka veteran, Colonel Oskar Dinort, and his Gruppe to brave the ground fire and attack the ships from low altitudes.

Flares dropped by German bombers illuminate the Kremlin on July 26, 1941. The Luftwaffe's attempt to raze it failed: Thick 17th Century roof tiles kept the incendiaries from doing much damage.

The dive-bombing attacks began on September 23. Among Dinort's pilots was a lieutenant named Hans-Ulrich Rudel, the son of a Silesian minister. Rudel, an avid sportsman who drank milk while others preferred schnapps, had been flying since 1938 but was considered so inept that a succession of commanders had kept him out of action until the Russian campaign. Rudel was determined to prove himself.

The primary targets were the battleships *October Revolution* and *Marat,* displacing 23,000 tons each and mounting a dozen 12-inch and sixteen 4.8-inch guns. On Rudel's first sortie he and the other Stuka pilots were blessed with heavy cloud cover over the target, which meant that they did not have to break out into the clear—and into the anti-aircraft fire—until they had penetrated the cloud base at 2,400 feet. Rudel kept the stick forward until the *Marat* filled his windscreen. Then he tripped the bomb-release button on the stick and pulled out almost at wave-top level. The bomb, a 1,000-pounder, struck the battleship's afterdeck and exploded in a sheet of flame. But the *Marat,* although badly damaged, was not finished.

Rudel would get a second chance, however, after Dinort ordered up special 2,000-pound bombs from Germany. They were so heavy that the Stukas could barely take off with them, but soon Rudel was back over Kronstadt, flying through a "brilliant blue sky, without a rack of cloud." Using the present tense as he relived the excitement of the moment, Rudel later described the mission: "We are still a few miles from our objective. I can already make out the *Marat* berthed in the harbor. The guns boom, the shells scream up at us, bursting in flashes of livid colors; the flak forms small fleecy clouds that frolic round us." Rudel then hurled his Ju 87 into a steep dive, following his squadron leader, a Lieutenant Steen, so closely that he could see "the horrified face of Steen's rear-gunner," who expected Rudel to "cut off his tail with my propeller and ram him." Rudel increased his dive angle to 90 degrees, whipped past Steen's Ju 87 and plunged straight for the *Marat* through a curtain of antiaircraft fire. "Now I press the bomb release switch on my stick and pull with all my strength. The height at which I have released my bomb is not more than 900 feet."

Coming out of the punishing dive, Rudel flashed across the water at an altitude of only 10 or 12 feet. Looking back, he saw a tremendous gout of flame from amidships. The huge bomb had crashed through the *Marat's* deck to explode in her magazine, splitting her in two.

After a few more raids on the Soviet Baltic Fleet, during which Rudel sank a cruiser, Dinort's Geschwader was abruptly withdrawn from the northern sector and sent southward to the Central Front to support the panzers in their last do-or-die attempt of 1941 to reach Moscow before the snows of the Russian winter halted offensive operations.

The gigantic attack by 66 German divisions was at first successful. Progress was soon slowed, however, by soaking autumn rains that bogged down the tanks in seas of mud and turned Luftwaffe forward airfields into quagmires. By October 30 the Germans were halted, still

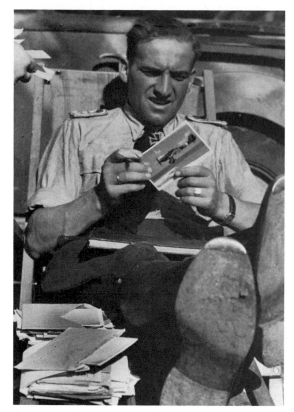

Stuka pilot Hans-Ulrich Rudel reads his mail between missions on a German airfield near Orel in Russia. Rudel, known as "the Eagle of the Eastern Front," destroyed three Soviet ships, 70 landing craft and 519 tanks. He flew 2,530 combat missions, the most by any pilot in any war.

40 miles from Moscow. When the first subfreezing temperatures hardened the roads and runways, the panzers rumbled forward again and by early December units of General Hermann Hoth's Third Panzer Group had reached the Volga Canal, 25 miles north of Red Square.

That was as close as the Germans got. Brutally cold weather stalled the tanks and grounded the planes. "Engines no longer start, everything is frozen stiff, no hydraulic apparatus functions, to rely on any technical instrument is suicide," wrote Rudel.

The situation rapidly worsened on December 6 when 100 fresh Soviet divisions, many transported 3,000 miles from Siberia—where they had been on guard against a possible Japanese attack from Manchuria—launched a surprise counteroffensive, breaking through the Wehrmacht's lines outside Moscow and hurling the Germans backward.

Near the town of Demyansk the situation quickly became critical: More than 100,000 Germans were encircled by the Russians. Now it was the Wehrmacht that was trapped, cut off from all supplies, and for the first time the Luftwaffe found itself cast in a purely defensive role. Germany's air arm was forced to become an airborne quartermaster corps, a mission it was ill equipped to carry out.

Nearly a quarter of the Luftwaffe's Ju 52 transports had been lost during the battle for Crete. The chief of Luftwaffe transport for Luftflotte 1, Colonel Fritz Morzik, carried only 220 Ju 52s on his roster and they had been used so hard that only 75 were flyable. Planes from other units along the front were called into play, a Gruppe was brought back from Sicily and crews just graduating from schools in Germany were hastily flown to Russia. Pilots with thousands of hours of air time found themselves sitting next to copilots who were still trying to find their way around the cockpit. Crewmen arrived from the scorching Libyan desert still wearing khaki and had to scrounge for woolen uniforms to protect against 40-below temperatures. In such inhuman cold the serviceability rate of Morzik's transport fleet dropped as low as 25 per cent; tires became brittle and cracked, radios proved useless and even 10-weight oil became as viscous as molasses.

Despite these seemingly impossible conditions, Morzik managed to supply the beleaguered troops at Demyansk, as well as 3,500 men trapped just to the south in Kholm. The Ju 52s were escorted by Me 109s, which successfully beat off the few Soviet fighters that attempted to oppose the shoestring airlift. The cost to the Luftwaffe was still high—265 Ju 52s, mostly victims of the brutal winter and Russian ground fire. By May 18, when the pockets were relieved, more than 160 trainloads of high-octane aviation fuel had been consumed. The airlift had succeeded, but barely, and the herculean efforts needed to keep it going were an indication that the Luftwaffe was spread thin.

While the bulk of the Luftwaffe was engaged in the struggle in Russia, some of its best units were fighting in North Africa, where Hitler had been forced once more to rescue his ally, Mussolini. There the German fliers performed brilliantly despite the baking sun and choking sand—and one fighter pilot emerged who blazed across the sky like a meteor. The ultimate result, however, was a catastrophe for the Axis partners, for the Luftwaffe and for the Wehrmacht as a whole.

The North African adventure began in 1940 when Mussolini, who dreamed of conquering the entire Middle East, ordered his troops in Libya to attack the British defending Egypt and the Suez Canal. But his poorly motivated and badly officered soldiers fared no better in Africa than they had in Greece. In December 1940 the Italian Army was routed by outnumbered but excellently led British forces. The Italians, cut off in huge pockets by fast-moving tanks, surrendered in droves. One British battalion commander jokingly put his bag at "five acres of officers and 200 acres of other ranks."

Furious as he was with the overambitious Mussolini, Hitler had but one choice—to shore up his ally's collapsing North African venture. Dispatched first, in March of 1941, were divisions of German tanks and infantry—the Afrika Korps—under the command of the brilliant panzer general of the Battle of France, Erwin Rommel. To give him initial air support, one Gruppe of Stukas, led by Colonel Walter Sigel, veteran of the French campaign, flew to Libya. When, as had happened during the Battle of Britain, Egyptian-based Hurricanes and Spitfires made mincemeat of the Ju 87s, Messerschmitt 109s of the now-famous Jagdgeschwader 27 were brought in, commanded by one of the Luftwaffe's top leaders, Captain Eduard Neumann.

Sigel's and Neumann's pilots provided Rommel with extraordinarily effective air support. They were at their finest in 1942 during the crucial battle for Libya's Bir Hacheim, a fortress some two miles square defended by General Pierre Koenig's 3,600-man 1st Free French Brigade. Koenig's troops occupied more than 1,000 camouflaged slit trenches, machine-gun posts, rifle pits and mortar positions. They slept in these holes, fought in them—and died in them.

The main assault on Bir Hacheim began on the morning of June 3 with a thundering bombardment by Sigel's Stukas and Rommel's 88-millimeter guns. Koenig's soldiers, many of whom were grizzled Foreign Legionnaires, took everything Rommel and the Luftwaffe could throw at them. Fourteen of Sigel's Stukas were shot down during a week of unrelenting combat. General Kesselring, brought from Russia to be in charge of the entire Mediterranean theater, added weight to the aerial assault by sending waves of Ju 88s from Greece and Crete to hammer Bir Hacheim. At one point the air was so obscured by flying sand and columns of smoke that a Stuka attack had to be called off because the airmen could not distinguish friend from foe. Not until June 10, after the Luftwaffe had flown 1,300 sorties against the fortress did the German infantry penetrate its outskirts.

The next morning more than 100 Stukas and 76 Junkers 88s swamped the French with 140 tons of bombs. His men exhausted and supplies of every kind running low, General Koenig had but one choice—to break out of Bir Hacheim with every soldier who could still fight. He led his surviving troops, 2,700 of them, crashing through the German-Italian lines, having accomplished a prodigy of defense that delayed Rommel's push toward the Nile for more than two weeks.

Among the fighter pilots who had helped defend the bombers over Bir Hacheim was Hans-Joachim Marseille *(pages 126-127)*, a Berliner of French descent, who had arrived in North Africa a year before the Bir Hacheim battle, at the age of 21, after serving his combat apprenticeship during the later stages of the Battle of Britain.

Marseille's previous commanding officers had found the young aviator an incorrigible prankster on the ground and in the air, but Eduard Neumann sensed that he had been given a great natural pilot and, aside from handing out an occasional fatherly lecture about reckless flying, let Marseille have his head. Marseille turned out to be a superb deflection, or off-angle, marksman. He did not need to get on the tail of an enemy plane to blast it from the sky. He could riddle a British fighter swooping across his Messerschmitt's path, leading it with his cannon and machine guns as a skeet shooter aims ahead of a speeding clay pigeon. Marseille was so good he could get off accurate deflection shots while his own 109 was in a roll, or while his quarry was executing frantic evasive maneuvers. His touch with stick and rudder was sure—he wore tennis shoes while flying for extra sensitivity on the rudder pedals—and he never skidded in turns. "His judgment of deflection was incredible," recalled his wingman, Sergeant Rainer Poettgen. "Each time he fired I saw his shells strike first the enemy's nose, then travel along to the cockpit. He wasted no ammunition."

This flying prodigy soon became the scourge of the RAF in North Africa. After warming up during the summer of 1941, Marseille had the first of many extraordinary days on September 24, shooting down five British planes. By February 1942 he had scored 48 victories. In 12 hectic minutes over Bir Hacheim in June, he destroyed six American-made Curtiss P-40 Tomahawks being flown by South Africans. In the seven days after Bir Hacheim's fall, as Rommel pushed on toward the Egyptian border, Marseille shot down another 20 RAF planes, raising his score to 101. At last, exhausted by the strain of constant combat, he was ordered home to Germany by Neumann and received the coveted Knight's Cross with Swords from the Führer himself.

After two months' leave, Marseille returned to Jagdgeschwader 27 as it was supporting Rommel's furious attack on the British Army's defensive positions at El Alamein, 240 miles inside Egypt. On September 1, 1942, Marseille's feats reached astonishing heights. The sky was alive with British fighters blasting Stukas. Marseille methodically shot down a pair of P-40s and a pair of Spitfires within 11 minutes. Refueled and rearmed, he returned to the air and between 10:55 and 11:05 a.m. sent eight P-40s to their destruction. That afternoon Marseille effortlessly chewed up another five of the hapless Curtiss fighters, making his score 17 kills for the day. On September 15, he ran his string to 150.

On September 26 Jagdgeschwader 27 tangled with Spitfires, and Marseille fought the longest dogfight of his career. The swirling, close-in combat lasted a full 15 minutes before he could get his sights where he wanted them. Then he pressed the firing button on his stick; cannon shells and 7.9-millimeter machine-gun slugs streaked unerringly backward along the Spitfire, and Marseille had another victory—his eighth since September 15, for a grand total of 158.

Four days later, when he was returning from a Stuka escort mission, he found his cockpit suddenly filling with smoke. He got on the radio immediately: "Elbe One. Smoke building up badly in cockpit. I can't see." The other members of the flight closed formation and steered him for home, encouraging Marseille to stick with it a few more minutes until they reached German lines. Clouds of black smoke were now billowing from the 109 and Marseille had no choice but to bail out. He flipped the hood open, turned the fighter on its back and fell free—only to have the slip stream blow him backward into the tail. He plummeted to the desert floor, his chute unopened. He was buried the next day, to be eulogized as "the unrivaled virtuoso among the fighter pilots of World War II" by Adolf Galland. Some people think he was the greatest who ever lived.

As if Marseille's death were a malign portent, the fortunes of the Afrika Korps rapidly declined after that. Unable to breach the British positions, Rommel's forces sat at El Alamein, at the end of overstretched supply lines. Then, beginning on October 23, the British, led by General

Ace Hans-Joachim Marseille thanks his ground crew for keeping his Me 109 in good flying order. During the 12 months in which he scored more than 150 kills over North Africa, his plane was not hit by a single enemy bullet.

Bernard Montgomery, smashed through the Afrika Korps defenses, destroyed some 450 German tanks and sent Rommel's battered troops reeling backward out of Egypt, across Libya and all the way to Tunisia. There they were backed up against fresh British and American forces that had landed in Morocco and Algeria in November 1942. Final catastrophe for the Axis forces in North Africa was not far off.

When fighting resumed in Russia in the spring of 1942, after the winter stalemate, the German Army and the Luftwaffe again tore enormous holes in the Soviet defenses and gobbled up immense stretches of the country. But since his forces were now stretched too thin to support a massive offensive along the entire front—the Wehrmacht had lost more than 750,000 men wounded and killed in 1941—Hitler decided to concentrate on the south. The targets: the great industrial city of Stalingrad on the distant Volga River, which produced many of the Red Army's tanks and other vehicles, the Soviet Union's main oil-producing region of the Caucasus and the great port of Sevastopol on the Black Sea. With these areas in German hands, Hitler thought, the Soviet war machine would be crippled for lack of equipment and fuel.

The air fighting in the summer of 1942 took on a new ferocity. The seemingly defunct Soviet Air Force had come back to life, equipped with a new generation of fighters, attack planes and medium bombers. The fighters were flawed aircraft. The MiG-3, although fast, had ma-

Axis troops form an honor guard for Hans Marseille's coffin, which was buried where the young flier fell to his death after an engine fire in his plane. All but four of Marseille's 158 victories were over enemy fighters, more elusive targets than bombers.

chine guns but no cannon. The Lavochkin (LaGG) 3, of wood-and-steel construction because aluminum was scarce, weighed more than 7,000 pounds and would snap into a vicious spin when turning. The Russian pilots detested the machine, with its lacquered plywood skin, and named it the "varnished guaranteed coffin." But the new planes, if far from ideal, were a distinct improvement over the antiquated machines of the year before—and thousands of them were coming off the production lines of the aircraft factories beyond the Urals.

Thousands were needed, it developed, since neither the Soviet pilots nor their planes were a match for the newest model of the Messerschmitt, the 109F. This version of the famous fighter was equipped with an improved 1,300-horsepower Daimler-Benz engine that gave it a top speed of 390 miles per hour. The previous model, the 109E, nicknamed Emil, the standard Messerschmitt of the air fighting over Britain, was about 35 miles per hour slower. Yet the 109F was still light and maneuverable. In the hands of such brilliant fliers as Major Gerhard Barkhorn, the 109F proved the scourge of the Soviet Air Force. His 109F, Barkhorn said, "could climb and turn like hell," and "I felt I could do anything with it." And indeed he could: Barkhorn shot down 301 planes over Russia—including Spitfires, Hurricanes and American-made Bell P-39 Aircobras sent to the Soviets by the Allies as military aid.

Such high scores by Luftwaffe fighter pilots in Russia were not unusual. Captain Emil Lang of Barkhorn's elite Jagdgeschwader 52 shot down 18 Soviet planes on one day, eclipsing Marseille's record by one. Lang went on to run his string to 173 before he was killed in combat. Captain Günther Rall, despite a near-fatal crash landing that fractured his spine in three places, ran his score to 275 confirmed kills. Rall bored right in on his victims, sometimes with spectacular results. Jumping one Russian fighter, he turned to port to open fire when the Soviet pilot heeled his own plane around. Rall's 109 smashed into the Russian from above "with an earsplitting, terrifying crash." The Russian's propeller sliced into Rall's fuselage while Rall's prop sawed through the LaGG's wing. The wing flew off and the plane spun to the ground. Rall nursed his crippled 109 back home, fearing that at any moment the fuselage would come apart in the air.

Rall was immediately given a new fighter, in which he had another close call. Attacking a Bell Aircobra, he struck with a fusillade of cannon and machine-gun fire. "There was a blinding sheet of fire as the fuel burned right in the tanks. This sheet of flame was at least 100 yards long and I had no choice but to fly right through it." Rall's 109 had fabric-covered ailerons, which vanished inside the fireball. He was able to nurse the plane home using rudder and elevators alone.

Germany's leading ace, Captain Erich Hartmann (pages 132-139), also of Jagdgeschwader 52, gunned down 352 Russian planes. Part of Hartmann's success lay in the fact that, like Rall, he got within almost suicidal range before pressing the trigger button. "I opened fire only when the whole windscreen was black with the enemy. Then not a

General Wolfram von Richthofen, commander of Fliegerkorps VIII during the Russian campaign, prepares to inspect front lines from an observation plane in 1942. A veteran of the Polish, French and Balkan fighting, he was the Luftwaffe's top expert on close air support of ground troops.

Atop an observation tower north of Sevastopol, Richthofen directs Luftwaffe bombing attacks against nearby Soviet forces in June of 1942. He was later promoted to field marshal and transferred from the Soviet Union to the Mediterranean front.

single shot goes wild.'' Hartmann got used to flying through the resulting debris; on eight separate occasions his 109 was so badly damaged by chunks of Soviet planes that Hartmann had to crash-land it.

Luftwaffe fighter pilots ran up such high scores not simply because they flew better equipment and there were always plenty of targets massed in the sky but also because they kept on flying. They flew until they were killed, captured or wounded so badly that they could never fly again. There was no magic number of missions to complete after which they could be sent home, as was the case, for example, with Americans. Hartmann flew 1,400 missions during the War and engaged in aerial combat 825 times.

The ferocity of the air and ground fighting reached a terrifying climax around Sevastopol on the Crimean peninsula. The strategic Black Sea port and its 110,000 inhabitants had been cut off by General Erich von Manstein's Eleventh Army since the autumn of 1941, but assaults against the thicket of Russian defensive positions ringing the city produced only heavy casualty lists. In the late spring of 1942 Manstein called in General Löhr's Luftflotte 4 to give air support to the 210,000 German and Rumanian troops besieging the city. Again Löhr turned to the dependable Richthofen and his Fliegerkorps VIII to help pulverize Sevastopol's defenses and attack the morale of the defenders with a ceaseless, crushing bombardment.

The shelling and bombing began on the morning of June 2, 1942. Richthofen's He 111s, Ju 88s and Stukas flew from dawn to dusk. ''Only after the sun had sunk below the horizon of the Black Sea was there a brief pause in the battle,'' recalled Colonel Hermann Plocher, a Luftwaffe staff officer who observed the action at Sevastopol. ''Then followed a brief period of deathlike sleep for the crew members, while nearby their engines were being replaced and tested with a deafening noise.'' During the day, after reconnaissance planes had skimmed low over the battlefield to pinpoint Soviet artillery and antiaircraft emplacements, Stukas screamed down to blast the Russian batteries.

Richthofen characteristically observed and directed the aerial bombardment from a raised platform so close to the Soviet airfields that he could easily see the clouds of dust being raised by Russian fighters revving up for takeoff. The moment the dust began to rise, batteries of the Luftwaffe's 88-millimeter flak guns would start throwing their high-velocity, flat-trajectory shells among the Soviet planes.

The tank and infantry assault against Sevastopol began on June 7. The ground troops were preceded by waves of low-flying bombers scouring every yard of the bitterly contested terrain. Stuka pilot Herbert Pabst remembers that ''at times it was hard to decide where to dive in to attack without ramming other aircraft.'' In spite of cloudless skies there was so much smoke and dust over Sevastopol that it was impossible to see even 300 feet. Strongpoint after strongpoint fell, followed finally, on July 1, by the city itself. All that was left in the end, said Pabst, were

An Me 109, upended in a crash near Stalingrad in 1942, perches beside a bombed-out building. During the height of the battle for the city, Luftwaffe planes

flew an average of 1,000 sorties a day against the defenders.

"immense mountains of debris." The German victory had been made possible by the close cooperation between German air and ground units. During the 30-day campaign Richthofen's fliers had logged a staggering 23,751 sorties—while losing only 31 aircraft. Never again would the Luftwaffe achieve such uncontested mastery of the air over an eastern battlefront.

Some 400 miles to the northeast General Friedrich von Paulus' huge Sixth Army of 20 divisions, including a panzer army, moved doggedly across the furnace-hot plains of southern Russia toward Stalingrad, another of Hitler's main 1942 objectives. The Sixth Army was slowed because much of the fuel needed by Paulus' tanks had been sent to General Ewald von Kleist's First Panzer Army for its long dash to the city of Rostov and from there into the distant Caucasus. By the time Paulus' advance units reached Stalingrad on August 23, the Soviets had been able to reinforce the city and build strong defenses amid its factories and apartment houses.

To soften up the city—and terrorize the population—General von Richthofen, fresh from the Crimea, launched a massive air assault on August 23, throwing in all 600 planes of his Fliegerkorps. This raid and the almost daily assaults that followed wrecked Stalingrad and killed many thousands of troops and civilians. But the Soviet soldiers just dug into the wreckage and fought back. Repeated efforts by Paulus' tanks and infantry to drive the last defenders out of Stalingrad's ruins and across the Volga were unavailing. With suicidal tenacity the Russian troops held on—then, as winter approached, they counterattacked.

Soviet Army pincers sliced in behind the Sixth Army, cutting through Paulus' thinly held flanks and surrounding his 300,000 men. Trapped in the Stalingrad pocket, Paulus considered trying to break out to the rear. Hitler forbade him to surrender even one inch of conquered territory. He must hold out until relieved. In the meantime, Göring had promised that the Luftwaffe would airlift in all the ammunition and food the trapped army would need, landing at two airfields within the pocket held by Paulus' troops. It was a repetition of the Demyansk airlift of the previous winter, but on a much larger scale. And now the Luftwaffe's supplies of pilots and of those old reliable transports, the Iron Annies, were running out.

Soon bitter winter storms so battered the Ju 52s and other aircraft pressed into duty as transports that by the end of November of 500 planes only some 125 were serviceable. They could airlift only a pitiful 20 per cent of the supplies Paulus' army needed. Again Göring had promised more than his men could conceivably deliver. ～

The ace of aces

For his prowess in a black-nosed Messerschmitt 109 *(right)*, the Soviets dubbed Luftwaffe pilot Erich Hartmann the "Black Devil of the Ukraine" and placed a 10,000-ruble price on his head. Because he arrived at the Eastern Front looking far younger than his 20 years, his fellow pilots nicknamed him *Bubi*, or "boy."

By either reckoning, Erich Hartmann, the top-scoring fighter ace of the entire War, was an enigma. Quiet and unassuming, he lacked the flamboyance of most fighter aces. Yet in only two and a half years—between October 1942 and May 1945—this modest hero accumulated a record-breaking total of 352 victories, rose to command Gruppe No. 1 of the Luftwaffe's most successful fighter wing, Jagdgeschwader 52, and earned one of Germany's most coveted military awards: the Knight's Cross of the Iron Cross with Oak Leaves, Swords and Diamonds *(right)*. His life story is told in his own photographs here and on the following pages.

The secret of Hartmann's success was summed up in his advice to young pilots, "Fly with your head, not with your muscles." Rejecting the strenuous thrust-and-parry tactics of traditional dogfighting as a waste of time and ammunition, he preferred to take his victim by surprise: He would bore in close and attack at point-blank range. A less skilled pilot would almost surely have collided with his adversary, but Hartmann possessed an uncanny knack for breaking away at the last possible second. In 825 instances of aerial combat, he was never wounded, and his plane was forced down only 16 times—and then often because it had been hit by debris from aircraft that Hartmann had destroyed.

The Soviets soon learned to steer clear of him. Like the other planes in Jagdgeschwader 52's Sweetheart Squadron, his Messerschmitt displayed a bleeding heart pierced by an arrow. But unlike them it bore his own distinctive marking, a black tulip that Hartmann had had painted on its nose. Forgoing a chance to go after the 10,000-ruble prize, Soviet formations would scatter whenever they spotted the tulip, and the Black Devil's tally leveled off accordingly. Only after Hartmann had the design painted out—and regained his anonymity—did he go on to achieve the score that set an all-time record.

Shown here with his wartime Me 109 and the Knight's Cross with Oak Leaves, Swords and Diamonds awarded him in 1944 as Germany's top ace, Major Erich Hartmann relaxes at a West German air base in 1959.

Erich Hartmann's mother, Elisabeth, herself an accomplished pilot, embarks on a flight in her Klemm L-20 sport plane.

Wearing his Hitler Youth uniform, 14-year-old Erich projects the clear-eyed determination of a future fighter ace.

A natural athlete and prizewinning skier, Hartmann leaps a snowdrift during a Hitler Youth competition in 1940.

From mother's glider to Me 109

From early childhood, Erich Hartmann displayed a remarkable affinity for flying, an interest that was encouraged by his mother. Elisabeth Hartmann was an enthusiastic pilot and the instructor of a boys' glider club, and had taught her son to fly a glider by the time he was 14. One year later, Erich, too, had become a licensed instructor—for the Glider Group of the Hitler Youth.

When Hartmann graduated from secondary school in 1940, he deferred his plans to become a doctor like his father and enlisted in the Luftwaffe. After basic training, he was assigned to become a fighter pilot. At gunnery school, his talent for marksmanship with an Me 109's machine guns amazed his superior officers. Then, when he was 20, he was posted to the Eastern Front.

Lying prone on a Baltic Sea beach, Hartmann (right) and another cadet engage in target practice during basic training.

Student pilots stretch out on a Luftwaffe airfield, the better to watch and analyze their comrades' takeoffs.

A proud cadet, Hartmann returns from his last flight at fighter-pilot school. Unlike later pilots, who were rushed into combat, he received 18 months of flight training before proceeding to the Eastern Front.

Midway through his training, Staff Sergeant Hartmann is reunited with his childhood sweetheart, Ursula Paetsch. They became engaged in 1943 and were married in 1944.

Upon his arrival at the Eastern Front, Hartmann slept in this tent.

Celebrating his first victory, Hartmann hoists his mechanic on his back.

Hartmann's crew chief, Heinz Mertens (left), became a close friend.

During a lull in the fighting, Lieutenant Hartmann (left) tackles a necessary chore—checking his clothing for lice.

Coming of age on the Eastern Front

Erich Hartmann's first air battle—over the Caucasus Mountains in October of 1942—was an almost unmitigated disaster. Flying as wingman to an experienced leader, he panicked, mistook his leader's Me 109 for a Russian fighter and fled. He climaxed the sortie by crash-landing, destroying his aircraft.

Chagrined, Hartmann set out to improve his performance. For the next few months, he flew with some of his squadron's best aces, observing their flying styles and evolving his own techniques. Gradually he trained himself to close to within 150 feet of the enemy before firing, the hazardous but sure-fire tactic that became his trademark.

On November 5, 1942, he made his first kill, and soon his score began to climb—90 downed planes by the end of August 1943, 115 a month later and 148 by the end of October, when he received the Knight's Cross. Higher orders of the award followed—the Oak Leaves after his 200th victory, in March 1944, the Swords after his 239th, in July, and the coveted Diamonds after his 301st, in August. With his 300th kill, Hartmann became the world's top-scoring ace.

On August 24, 1944, Hartmann—with 296 kills—prepares for takeoff.

Friends await word of Hartmann's 300th victory.

As his squadronmates wave and cheer, Hartmann waggles his wing tips to signal his 300th downed plane. In two sorties that day, he destroyed 11 Russian aircraft, bringing his total score to 301 victories.

Framed by a makeshift victory wreath, Hartmann reacts to the taste of warm champagne. In their haste to drink a toast to his record-breaking sortie, his fellow pilots did not bother to chill the bottle.

Hitler congratulates Lieutenant Hartmann after presenting him with the Diamonds to his Knight's Cross.

At an airfield outside Berlin, Hartmann confers with General Adolf Galland and Reich Marshal Göring in January 1945.

A consummate pilot right to the end

When awarding Hartmann the Knight's Cross with Oak Leaves, Swords and Diamonds, Hitler told him that he was now too important to be risked in combat on the Eastern Front. Therefore he was being transferred to a special fighter unit that was testing the revolutionary new twin-engined jet fighter, the Me 262.

But Hartmann believed that he could best serve his country in its desperate fight against the Soviets, and he managed to persuade Göring to cancel his orders and return him to active service in the East. Göring complied, and Hartmann soon became the commander of Gruppe No. 1 of Jagdgeschwader 52. Leading his pilots in their final defense of the retreating German Army, he raised his tally of victories to 352.

When Germany fell to the Allies on May 8, 1945, Hartmann surrendered to the Americans. They handed him over to the Russians, and he was sent to a prison camp deep within the Soviet Union.

Back at the Eastern Front, Hartmann beams after pushing his score to 350.

In a Soviet prison camp, Hartmann writes to his wife. This letter was eventually smuggled into West Germany by a friend.

During a visit to the United States in 1961, Hartmann test-flies an American F-106 supersonic fighter aircraft.

A new life in a postwar world

Held captive in Soviet prison camps for 10½ years, Hartmann found that he was sorely tested. At first, he was offered a position in the East German air force. He refused. He was then sentenced to 25 years' hard labor.

Finally, in 1955, West Germany effected his release, and Hartmann returned home to a hero's welcome. Three years later, he was chosen to command the West German air force's first all-jet fighter wing. As the leader of Jagdgeschwader 71, Hartmann made several visits to the United States. There, while learning to fly the latest U.S.-built jets, the ace of aces shared with the young American fighter pilots the priceless experience of his 825 air battles.

Hartmann attends a 1961 military ceremony with General Josef Kammhuber, the inventor of the Luftwaffe's Kammhuber defense system during World War II.

At an airfield in Germany late in the War, ground crewmen ready a Messerschmitt 110 fighter for a night sortie against Allied bombers.

5

The air war over Germany

From the beginning of 1943 it began to be apparent that Germany's fortunes were turning on all fronts. The Reich was paying for overextending its forces, and the Luftwaffe was stuck with a large share of the bill. The reversals assumed staggering proportions. On February 2, the chewed-up remnant of the 300,000-man force encircled at Stalingrad surrendered. The Luftwaffe had concentrated some 850 planes in the Stalingrad supply operation and had lost 488 of them. Among them were aircraft pulled in from training duty and bomber forces, including 100 He 111s transferred from the Mediterranean theater. After counting up the losses Göring observed: "There died the core of the German bomber fleet."

The news from North Africa soon proved equally discouraging. In mid-May 250,000 Axis soldiers surrendered to the British and Americans in Tunisia. The Luftwaffe, which had lost some 2,400 aircraft in that region in the preceding seven months, withdrew the last of its North African forces to Sicily. Two months later, when the Allies crossed the Mediterranean and invaded that Italian island, the Luftwaffe retreated to mainland Italy—leaving behind the wreckage of 600 planes destroyed by Allied bombing raids.

But the most persistent indication that all was far from well—despite the efforts of the Propaganda Ministry to make it seem otherwise—was the pounding that Germany was now taking from Allied bombs. For months British bombers had been roaring across the North Sea almost nightly to attack Germany. In February the United States Eighth Air Force, operating from England, had commenced regular daylight raids; soon the Allied invasion of the Reich's airspace had become a round-the-clock insult to the Luftwaffe. And before the year was out bombers from America's Fifteenth Air Force, based first in North Africa and later in Italy, would be flying up from the south to add their might to the punishment Germany was taking.

During the first half of 1943, the Luftwaffe's morale started to crumple beneath a growing sense of futility. One of the greatest barriers to an adequate defense of the homeland, many officers believed, was Hitler's and Göring's insistence that the air force was primarily an offensive weapon. On the Führer's orders aircraft factories concentrated on producing bombers rather than fighters. Now, with most of the best planes and pilots committed elsewhere, the defense of the Reich suffered from a lack of men and equipment.

The night-fighter arm began the year with some 390 aircraft, mostly twin-engined Me 110s, with which to fend off enemy raiding forces that were often twice that large. The day-defense force was even more heavily outnumbered, with only about 200 single-engined fighters to throw against the American bombers. However, it did have generally excellent aircraft, including not only the Me 109 but the newer Focke-Wulf 190. The A-3 model of the Fw 190, introduced only the year before, was driven by a 1,700-horsepower radial engine that gave the fighter a top speed of 418 miles per hour, and the new plane was unmatched in maneuverability. It was a fine airplane, but there were not enough of them.

"For two years we had been on a wrong track," said General Adolf Galland. "After the Battle of Britain we should have switched over to defense in the west. We should have given the fighter priority over the bomber, as the British had done when they were threatened by the German raids, before they took the offensive again. Only the reestablishment of air superiority over our own territory would put us into the position that one day would allow us to resume the offensive."

Hitler's attitude toward defensive needs was amply demonstrated in the spring of 1943, when Major General Josef Kammhuber, the Luftwaffe's chief of night-defense fighters, proposed that his force be expanded to more than 2,100 aircraft. Kammhuber convinced Göring that the expansion had merit, but Hitler would not hear of it. Nor would he listen to Kammhuber's argument that Germany would soon be in even worse trouble because the Allied air forces were growing so rapidly. The Americans, Kammhuber contended, were supplying their air force with 5,000 new planes a month.

"It's absolute nonsense!" Hitler retorted. "If the figures were right, you'd be right, too. In that case, I should have to withdraw from the Eastern Front forthwith, and apply all resources to air defense. But they are *not* right! I will not stand for such nonsense!"

At this point in the discussion, Göring abruptly turned on his subordinate and joined Hitler's tantrum, berating the astonished Kammhuber for making "idiotic requests." Kammhuber, Göring said, was making him look like an ass with all these self-aggrandizing proposals. "You want to have the whole Luftwaffe," sneered Göring; "why don't you sit right down in my chair?"

But during the next few months, as Allied bombing raids increased in frequency and effectiveness and anxiety mounted among Luftwaffe officers, Göring at last agreed that something had to be done. In August he called his leading commanders to a meeting at the Wolf's Lair, Hitler's command post in East Prussia, and announced a dramatic turnabout in policy. The Luftwaffe, he said, would henceforth shift over to the defensive. Lest anyone think he was giving up hopes of victory, Göring quickly added that under the protection of its concentrated defensive forces the Luftwaffe would soon recover the strength to attack

A Luftwaffe V-1 rocket—one of Hitler's so-called vengeance weapons—soars from its launching pad toward Great Britain. The V-1 accounted for the deaths of 6,000 Londoners and the wounding of 40,000 more during the summer of 1944.

again. All those present supported the decision. Galland said afterward that "never before and never again did I witness such determination and agreement among the circle of those responsible for the leadership of the Luftwaffe."

Armed with this consensus, Göring next took his proposal to Hitler for approval. While Göring conferred with the Führer, Galland and the others could only sit and wait and hope that Hitler could be persuaded. "In this hour," Galland wrote later, "the fate of the Luftwaffe was decided."

Suddenly the door flew open and an ashen Göring hurried through the room. Without speaking a word, he disappeared into an adjacent private office. Hitler, explained Göring's shocked chief aide, who had attended the meeting, had rejected outright any notion of going onto the defensive.

When Galland and Dietrich Peltz, commander of combat fighters, were at last summoned into the inner office, they found that the Reich Marshal had collapsed emotionally. "His head buried in his arms on the table, he moaned some indistinguishable words," Galland recalled later. "We stood there in embarrassment. At last Göring pulled himself together and said we were witnessing his deepest moments of despair. The Führer had lost faith in him. The Führer had announced that the Luftwaffe had disappointed him too often. A change-over from offensive to defensive in the air against the west was out of the question. Now as before the motto was still: Attack!" Moreover, Göring now declared that Hitler was right. The Luftwaffe would continue with the series of bombing attacks against England that it had launched a few months earlier—though these "Baby Blitz" raids rarely included more than 100 German bombers—and there would be no new emphasis on developing the defensive fighter forces.

Still, although Hitler never really brought his mental image of the Luftwaffe as an offensive weapon into line with the War's changing reality, the pressure of urgent necessity ultimately transformed the air force into what amounted to a defensive arm. When Germany first attacked Russia in June 1941, more than half the power of the Luftwaffe had been devoted to supporting the invasion. But by late 1943, less than one fifth of the Luftwaffe's strength was concentrated on the Eastern Front. Most of it was devoted instead to defending the Reich from the British and American bombers.

The foundations for the Luftwaffe's defense of the Reich had been laid early in the War. In June of 1940, soon after the RAF began to make its nightly incursions into German airspace, Göring established a night-fighter organization in the Luftwaffe to counteract the British raids. To head the night fighters, Göring selected Josef Kammhuber. He soon proved to have a special genius for devising complex electronic ambushes for the enemy.

Kammhuber set up a radar fence that by March 1941 stretched across western Germany from the Danish border to the Rhine estuary in Holland. Known to the enemy as the Kammhuber Line, it consisted of overlapping zones called "boxes," each covering roughly 20 miles of the line. Inside each of these boxes there was a station controlling a single night fighter—most often an Me 110—that lurked like a spider waiting for its prey to jiggle the web: When an enemy bomber approached the box, up went the fighter, guided by the control station's radar. In addition to two short-range radar sets, one for tracking the intruder, one for tracking the night fighter so that its pilot could be led to his quarry, each installation had a long-range radar set for early warning, capable of reaching out 75 miles or more.

The Luftwaffe called each box of the line a *Himmelbett* (literally heavenly bed), the German term for a four-poster. Each *Himmelbett* control station could direct only one fighter at a time, and since the average interception took about 10 minutes, a station and a fighter could engage no more than about six intruders an hour. This was sufficient during the early phase of Britain's air offensive, when the bomber crews picked their own routes to their targets and entered German airspace at widely scattered points. But beginning with an

MAJOR GENERAL JOSEF KAMMHUBER

A radar network for night defense

When the RAF began night raids against Germany in 1940, the Luftwaffe countered with a defense system that became known to the Allies by the name of its organizer, night-fighter chief Major General Josef Kammhuber.

Eventually stretching 650 miles from Denmark through eastern France, the Kammhuber Line was a thorny hedge of radar and fighter installations, flak batteries and ground observers, all linked by telephone to local command posts.

In each post, the radar-tracked paths of an enemy bomber and a pursuing night fighter were plotted with beams of light on a frosted-glass table *(right)*. The Luftwaffe pilot was then vectored in for the kill by radio.

Each post in turn reported to one of seven Luftwaffe control centers, where officers could ascertain the overall battle situation from a screen showing all aircraft positions *(far right)*.

A long-range Freya radar tower, flanked by short-range precision Würzburg radar dishes, scans the sky for approaching bombers.

Color-coded light beams—red for an enemy bomber, blue for a German fighter—projected onto a glass plotting table made interceptions possible.

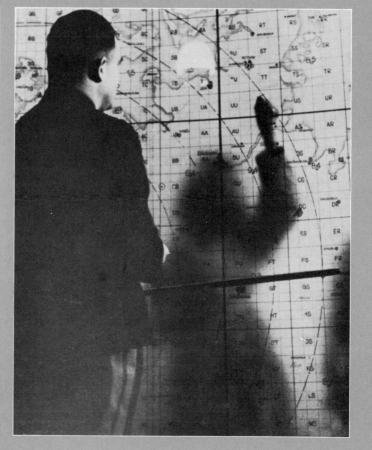

A Luftwaffe liaison officer inspects a battle situation on a translucent control center map as aircraft positions—called in from Kammhuber Line stations—are plotted on the back by women aides.

attack of unprecedented size on Cologne in May 1942—the first 1,000-bomber raid—the British massed their aircraft into bomber streams that overwhelmed the fighter-directing stations with numbers. For every bomber that was downed en route to Cologne, more than 20 safely penetrated the Kammhuber Line.

Kammhuber responded by adding new zones, thus deepening his line; now the enemy planes had to pass through box after box to reach their targets. By mid-1943 the Kammhuber Line was a gigantic game board; British bomber pilots trying to carry their bombs to goal played for their lives against ground observers, searchlights, radar-directed night fighters and radar-controlled flak batteries. But the British were able to maintain their losses at an acceptable level that their aircraft industry could keep up with, largely because they matched every German technological advance with one of their own.

Each side had its own competitive and ingenious corps of physicists, engineers and technicians working to equip its pilots with the latest electronic guidance and warning systems. These backroom wizards laced the skies over western Europe with invisible electronic homing beams, radar probes and infrared sensors. After the British devised electronic guidance systems named Gee and Oboe to direct bombers to their targets, the Germans countered with jamming devices that swamped the British signals and rendered them almost useless over German territory. At the same time, the British were jamming radio traffic between the *Himmelbett* control stations and the German night fighters. The German answer was to rely on radar units aboard the fighters themselves to guide the pilots to their prey.

Before long Luftwaffe night-fighter pilots discovered that the very radar guiding them to kills in fact often betrayed them. English escort fighters armed with a tracking unit called Serrate could home in on the German airborne radar beams with devastating results. One especially clever British device, called Perfectos, could reach out electronically and turn on an identification signal that Luftwaffe fighters used to enable German ground radar to distinguish them from enemy aircraft. In effect, Perfectos made German planes declare their whereabouts just when the Luftwaffe pilots wanted most to remain concealed. German engineers, meanwhile, had in turn devised homing devices called Flensburg and Naxos-Z that enabled Luftwaffe pilots to track in on the distinctive signals emitted by British airborne radar.

In this deadly game of cat-and-mouse, old-fashioned trickery also played a part. To mislead British bomber pilots, the Germans constructed giant decoys that from the air looked like cities, complete with beckoning factory stacks, and sent aloft flares similar to the markers dropped by the Pathfinder pilots who led bombers to their targets. At times the British fed a welter of fake instructions into the Luftwaffe's communications system instead of jamming it. When this technique, called Operation *Corona,* was first used in the fall of 1943, an enraged German

Frontline fighters of the Reich

The four sleek interceptors shown on these pages represent highlights in the remarkable 10-year evolution of Luftwaffe fighters.

The earliest, Willy Messerschmitt's Me 109 monoplane fighter, was first flown in 1935; it was such an innovative design that it shocked Germany's military planners, who still thought in terms of the open-cockpit biplanes of World War I. A twin-engined fighter, the Me 110, built for long-range operations, followed a year later. The Focke-Wulf 190, introduced in 1939, was a high-performance fighter plane with a top speed of more than 400 mph. And the Me 262, unveiled during the waning months of the War, represented a major technological breakthrough: It was the first jet to engage in aerial combat.

Of the four depicted, all but the Me 262 are late models; the years they entered service are in parentheses. The Me 109, Me 110 and Fw 190 have been rendered to scale; the Me 262 is shown in slightly larger proportion.

MESSERSCHMITT ME 109 E-4 (1940)
A heavily armed interceptor with all-metal stressed-skin construction, the Me 109 was originally capable of 290 mph but was gradually improved: The E-4 model reached 354 mph. More Me 109s were produced than any other German fighter— approximately 35,000 in all.

MESSERSCHMITT ME 110 G-4 (1942)
Though a dismal failure in its role as a long-range escort fighter, the Me 110 proved its worth flying defensive missions at night. It carried radar, eñabling it to "see" in the dark, and upright 20-mm. cannon in the cockpit that could be fired at enemy bombers from directly underneath.

FOCKE-WULF FW 190 A8/U6 (1943)
In 1941, with German fighter supremacy being challenged by the British Spitfires, the Luftwaffe raised the ante by deploying the Focke-Wulf 190—a masterpiece of warplane design. The new interceptor was able to fly higher and farther than the fabled Messerschmitt 109.

MESSERSCHMITT ME 262 A-1A (1944)
*Ahead of its time but too late to stem the
flow of Allied bombers over Germany, the
Messerschmitt 262 had a top speed of
540 mph. About 1,400 of the jets were
produced before the end of the War. This
one was attached to General Adolf Galland's
elite fighter squadron, Jagdverband 44.*

ground control officer, hearing his orders countered in perfect German by an unknown voice, cursed exasperatedly into his microphone. This prompted the quick-witted British radio interloper to sow more confusion by declaring: "The Englishman is now swearing." "It is not the Englishman who is swearing," the despairing German pleaded with his pilots. "It is I."

Two technological developments—one German, one British—that had immense impact on the battle over the Reich did not depend on electronic gadgets at all but were the result of mechanical ingenuity. One was the simple expedient of mounting a pair of 20-millimeter cannon almost upright in the fuselage of a night fighter. Since they were aimed upward, a night-fighter pilot was able to slip up beneath an unsuspecting bomber and fire away—taking care to hit the fuel tanks and not the bomb bay, since an explosion of the bombload might destroy his own aircraft. The new upward-firing cannon were dubbed *Schräge Musik* (literally, slanting music), German for "jazz."

Devastating as their *Schräge Musik* was, the men of the Luftwaffe found their entire defense system nearly crippled by a new British invention, introduced at about the same time, that was at once even simpler and more effective: slivers of paper about a foot long and a half inch wide, faced on one side with aluminum foil and known by the code name Window. When scattered in the air, a bundle of 2,000 slivers would send back a radar echo resembling a bomber's. Starting in mid-1943, the British used some 250 million strips of Window every week to sow near-total confusion in the German airspace and on the ground.

On the night of July 24, 1943, the Luftwaffe encountered Window for the first time during a big British raid on Hamburg. As 746 bombers crossed the Channel, they began strewing the sky with strips of aluminum foil. On the radar screens below, the operators saw what appeared to be an approaching force of no fewer than 11,000 planes. It could not be true, but there it was, on the cathode-ray tube. As the puzzled night-fighter pilots aloft listened, wondering what kind of madness had gripped their controllers, the airwaves were filled with a chaos of strange and conflicting communications: "Try without your ground control!" "It is impossible! Too many hostiles!" "The enemy are reproducing themselves!"

Pilots with their own airborne radar began searching the skies and found themselves as startled and perplexed as the controllers below. Because a slowly falling cloud of Window remained relatively stationary in the air, the radar echo returning from it reflected the speed of the night fighter, creating the illusion that the nonexistent enemy aircraft were moving at an extraordinary velocity. One Luftwaffe flier recalled later that he was delighted when his radio operator, a man named Facius, found the first blip on his radar. "I swung round onto the bearing. Facius proceeded to report three or four targets on his screens. I hoped that I would have enough ammunition to deal with them!

"Then Facius suddenly shouted, 'Tommy flying toward us at a great

speed! Distance decreasing—2,000 meters . . . 1,500 . . . 1,000 . . . 500 . . . '

"I was speechless. Facius already had a new target. 'Perhaps it was a German night fighter on a westerly course,' I said to myself, and made for the next bomber. It was not long before Facius shouted again, 'Bomber coming for us at a hell of a speed—2,000 . . . 1,000 . . . 500 . . . he's gone!' " 'You're crackers, Facius,' I said jokingly. But I soon lost my sense of humor, for this crazy performance was repeated a score of times."

Aided by Window's radar-befuddling rain, the British bombers went on to inflict upon Hamburg the first of a devastating series of raids. The foil strips also threw into confusion the operators of the sophisticated radar guidance systems controlling the 22 searchlight batteries and 54 flak installations guarding the city. The bombers arrived over Hamburg to find the skies ablaze with an unforgettable display as the searchlights and flak guns, responding to the same electronic will-o'-the-wisps that had so confused radio operator Facius, sprayed the empty air with shellbursts and wildly playing light beams. While the Germans flailed at nonexistent targets, most of the real bombers slipped through the defenses. The raiders did extensive damage to Hamburg's utilities, industry and homes, and suffered a loss of only 12 planes—a casualty rate of just 1.5 per cent. They struck Hamburg again two nights later. This time the blazing city was swept by a fire storm as the updraft of

Searchlights seeking out attacking British bombers and tracers from flak batteries streak the sky over a north German city in 1941. As soon as the altitude of an enemy formation was determined, Luftwaffe antiaircraft gunners would preset their shells to burst at the bombers' level.

rising heat from burning structures sucked in air to feed the combustion, incinerating buildings and inhabitants in temperatures of more than 1,800 degrees. It was, said the city's despondent police chief afterward, "a fire typhoon such as was never before witnessed, against which every human resistance was quite useless." More than 40,000 Germans died that night.

"Give us another five or six attacks like those on Hamburg," said Göring's deputy, Erhard Milch, after the city had been hit four more times in July and August, "and the German people will just give up, no matter how strong-willed they are. The people will say: 'We've had enough, we simply cannot take any more.' The man at the front will have to dig himself a hole and stay in it until the attackers have gone away. What the homeland is having to suffer, that is appalling."

A possible solution to the Window problem had been indicated some months earlier by Major Hajo Herrmann, the ace bomber pilot who had been the hero of the raid on the Greek port of Piraeus in April 1941. Herrmann, now assigned to the Luftwaffe staff college, argued that night fighters could overcome British electronic trickery if they did not depend on radar or radios for guidance but stalked the bombers in a free chase. Instead of being tethered in Kammhuber Line boxes, the high-flying fighters would follow the enemy to his target, where the combined illumination of searchlights and flames from burning buildings would silhouette the bombers from below. To avoid destroying the German planes, flak batteries would set the fuses of their shells to explode at no higher than 15,000 feet; the fighters would operate above that level. Because they would not need to carry an abundance of heavy electronic gear, single-engined aircraft, faster and more maneuverable than the Me 110s, could be employed.

Kammhuber had opposed the idea as a step backward from his sophisticated radar-control system, but Herrmann had gone over his head to win approval for a small test. After the Hamburg disaster, Göring authorized the creation of a Geschwader that included some 60 Messerschmitt 109s and Focke-Wulf 190s, to try out Herrmann's idea. Because of their free-roving style of attack these night fighters would be known as Wild Boars.

Meanwhile, the Me 110 night fighters that were the workhorses of the now-crippled *Himmelbett* system would use a modified form of Herrmann's Wild Boar tactics. They would be guided to the vicinity of approaching bombers by ground controllers, who were beginning to extrapolate from the Window blips on their radar screens where the real enemy was likely to be. Once in the area of the bombers, the Me 110 pilots, too, would follow, using their airborne radar if Window permitted and visual contact with the enemy planes if it did not. They were called Tame Boars.

Wild Boars and Tame Boars proved themselves on the night of August 23, when 727 Window-strewing British bombers attacked Berlin. The bomber pilots, who were accustomed to contending only with flak once they were over a target, were startled to find the sky over Berlin swarming with Focke-Wulfs and Messerschmitts. Fifty-six bombers were shot down—a loss rate of almost 8 per cent, higher than the British could sustain over a lengthy period—and another 31 were damaged. During two follow-up raids on Berlin on August 31 and September 3, the night fighters achieved similar scores. In the three attacks the British did extensive damage to the capital but failed to obliterate it as they had hoped, and in the process lost 123 bombers.

In the meantime, the Americans, too, were discovering that the Luftwaffe was still a formidably dangerous enemy—particularly when confronted in broad daylight. The British had tried to dissuade the United States from daytime raids against Germany, predicting that the losses would be too high to sustain for long, but the Americans believed that only daylight bombing would guarantee the kind of pinpoint accuracy necessary to destroy Hitler's industrial base. The fighters that escorted the B-17 Flying Fortresses and B-24 Liberators of the United States Eighth Air Force on missions could fly only 160 to 175 miles before having to turn back, but this did not stop the Americans from mounting an attack deep into Germany on August 17, 1943. The mission was a double strike: 147 Flying Fortresses would attack a Messerschmitt factory at Regensburg; another 216 would bomb a ball-bearing production complex at Schweinfurt. To get to Regensburg, the bomb-

On a night raid over Germany, a British Lancaster bomber with one engine shot away is silhouetted against flares and smoke. Luftwaffe pilots could synchronize the speed of their twin-engined fighters with that of the Lancasters, fly underneath them and stay there—unseen by the bombers' crews—until ready to attack.

ers would have to journey 300 miles over enemy territory without fighter protection; those flying to Schweinfurt would have a somewhat shorter but scarcely less dangerous trip.

The Luftwaffe day fighters struck soon after the American escorts reached their range limit and turned around. The fury of the German attack was later described by an American flier, Colonel Beirne Lay, copilot of one of the Fortresses in the lowermost portion of the rear combat wing, which took the brunt of the onslaught:

"Swinging their yellow noses around in a wide U-turn, a 12-ship squadron of Me 109's came in from 12 to 2 o'clock in pairs and fours, and the main event was on. A shining silver object sailed over our right wing, I recognized it as a main exit door. Seconds later, a dark object came hurtling through the formation, barely missing several props. It was a man, clasping his knees to his head, revolving like a diver in a triple somersault. I didn't see his chute open.

"A B-17 turned gradually out of the formation to the right, maintaining altitude. In a split second the B-17 completely disappeared in a brilliant explosion, from which the only remains were four small balls of fire, the fuel tanks, which were quickly consumed as they fell earthward. Our airplane was endangered by falling debris. Emergency hatches, exit doors, prematurely-opened parachutes, bodies, and assorted fragments of B-17's and Hun fighters breezed past us in the slipstream."

The raiders who struck at Schweinfurt had to run the gantlet again on their way back to England, while the Regensburg force continued south, escaping across the Alps to American bases in North Africa. Sixty bomb-

His night-camouflaged Me 109 having been checked out by his ground crew, a Luftwaffe pilot prepares to prowl the sky for bombers in 1944. Such free-roving fighters, called Wild Boars, first proved their worth by downing 12 British bombers over Cologne on July 3, 1943.

ers were shot down out of a total of 363 and another 55 were damaged beyond repair when they crash-landed in North Africa. The Luftwaffe lost a scant 25 fighters.

Although it did not always manage to exact so painful a toll from enemy raiders, and sometimes suffered heavy losses of its own, the Luftwaffe continued intermittently throughout the autumn of 1943 to make the Allies pay for their intrusions. When American bombers struck Schweinfurt again on October 14, the day fighters and flak claimed 60 Flying Fortresses out of a force of 291, while the Germans lost just 38 fighters.

The night fighters, now using the Wild and Tame Boar system as standard procedure (Kammhuber, who had opposed it, was removed from his command and shunted off to oblivion in Scandinavia in November), ran their string of successes well into the new year. By now the airborne radar operators of the Tame Boars had become adept at distinguishing between the blips on their screens that meant Window and those that represented bona fide aircraft; moreover, the bombers often came in such massive numbers that the fighter pilots could hardly have avoided them if they wished to.

One Tame Boar radar operator, a Sergeant Ostheimer, later described such an encounter with an 88-mile-long stream of 648 Lancaster and Halifax bombers en route to Magdeburg, near Berlin, on the night of January 21, 1944. Ostheimer was in a twin-engined Ju 88 piloted by an aristocratic officer, Major Prince Heinrich zu Sayn-Wittgenstein. The Prince, one of the Luftwaffe's leading aces, already had 79 kills to his credit. His aircraft was equipped with *Schräge Musik,* the upward-firing cannon that enabled him to slip in under his victims and dispatch them without being seen. Because *Schräge Musik* fired no tracers, the crews of the bombers being attacked and their comrades in nearby planes often had no idea where the fire was coming from.

"At about 22:00 hours I picked up the first contact," recalled Ostheimer. "It was a Lancaster. We moved into position and opened fire, and the aircraft immediately caught fire in the left wing. It went down at a steep angle and started to spin. Between 22:00 and 22:05 hours the bomber crashed and went off with a violent explosion.

"Again we searched. At times I could see as many as six aircraft on my radar. The next target was sighted: again a Lancaster. Following the first burst from us there was a small fire, and the machine dropped back its left wing and went down in a vertical dive. Shortly afterward I saw it crash. It was sometime between 22:10 and 22:15 hours.

"After a short interval we again sighted a Lancaster. There was a long burst of fire and the bomber ignited and went down. I saw it crash sometime between 22:25 and 22:30 hours.

"Immediately afterward we saw yet another four-motored bomber. After one firing pass this bomber went down in flames; at about 22:40 hours I saw the crash."

Four enemy bombers within 40 minutes—an incredible score. But

Ostheimer was soon to receive a jolt. "Yet again I had a target on my search equipment. We again sighted a Lancaster and after one attack it caught fire in the fuselage. The fire then died down and we moved into position for a new attack." Apparently at that moment a British gunner sighted the Ju 88. "Major Wittgenstein was ready to shoot when, in our own machine, there were terrible explosions and sparks. It immediately caught fire in the left wing and began to go down. The canopy above my head flew away and I heard on the intercom a shout of 'Get out!'" Ostheimer tore off his oxygen mask and helmet and parachuted safely to the ground, but Wittgenstein, now with 83 victories to his credit, went down with his plane. The British lost 55 bombers in the Magdeburg raid.

The night fighters achieved their most spectacular success—the greatest Luftwaffe defensive triumph of the entire War—on the night of March 30, 1944. That evening 795 Allied bombers—a few American planes were included in the preponderantly British force—set off for a raid on Nuremberg, where factories were turning out tanks, armored cars and diesel engines. The pilots expected to have cloud cover along the way as protection from the night fighters. Instead the sky was clear and moonlit. And because the night was exceptionally cold, the big aircraft trailed wakes of long white contrails.

At the first report of an oncoming bomber stream, 246 night fighters took off from bases throughout Germany. Tame Boars from the 3rd Fighter Division were ordered to rendezvous around a combination radio-and-visual beacon, code-named Ida, southwest of Cologne, that lay squarely in the path of the bomber stream. As the bombers ran head on into the swarm of waiting night fighters, the Luftwaffe pilots began shooting them out of the sky at the phenomenal rate of one every minute. The pilot of one Lancaster warned his crew, "Better put your parachutes on, chaps; I've just seen the forty-second one go down."

As the bombers that made it past Ida turned southward toward Nuremberg, word of their new course was flashed to the 1st and 2nd Fighter Divisions, whose aircraft were directed to intercept them. Each of the bombers was dropping Window at the rate of two bundles per minute after the turn toward Nuremberg, but the foil posed little problem for the night fighters wheeling through the bright sky—they downed 10 more bombers in the 75-mile stretch between the turn and Nuremberg. Another 39 bombers were shot down over the city.

"Normally our biggest problem was to find the bomber stream," said Lieutenant Helmut Schulte, "but on this night we had no trouble." Schulte proceeded to down four bombers while firing just 56 rounds from his cannon. The Luftwaffe's high scorer of the evening was Lieutenant Martin Becker, a veteran pilot. Becker's Me 110 was not equipped with *Schräge Musik,* but it took him just 30 minutes to destroy three Halifaxes and three Lancasters. He had to land to refuel but took off again and, as the Allies headed for home, downed a seventh British bomber.

The destruction was surprisingly one-sided. Lieutenant Fritz Lau,

Victim of a lone Focke-Wulf 190 fighter seen wheeling in the distance, a B-17 bomber that strayed from its formation loses altitude near Bremen in November 1943. Early in the War American bombers were unprotected once they were deep inside Germany; in 1944, they received fighter escort all the way to the target.

racing toward the action from his base at Athies, France, was able to locate the bomber stream from a distance by the burning planes he saw plummeting to earth. Because German aircraft had many parts that contained magnesium, they blazed bright white as they fell, while British planes burned a dark red. "On this night," Lau said afterward, "I only saw two white fires, but many red ones." Only about 10 German aircraft were destroyed. The raiding force of 795 bombers lost 94 planes. The loss in Allied bomber crewmen was staggering: 545 dead and some 200 wounded.

On learning of the damage inflicted on the Nuremberg raiders, Göring exulted in "the admirable bravery of the night-fighter crews that has brought about a new triumph over the British" and said: "Let us have still more." But the dark red flames of falling British bombers on the night of March 30 did not signal the advent of further victory for the Luftwaffe. Never again would the German air force inflict such a defeat on its enemies. From now on, it would be fighting for survival.

For despite the string of nighttime Luftwaffe victories, the air war had already taken a decisive turn in favor of the Allies—a turn that was abundantly evident to the German pilots who fought by the revealing light of day. There now appeared in the skies over Germany a new American aircraft, the P-51B Mustang. Manufactured by North American Aviation Incorporated, this improved version of an earlier, lackluster P-51 had a 1,400-horsepower V-12 engine that gave it a top speed of 440 miles per hour. The Mustang was more than 30 miles an hour faster than the Me 109, some 20 miles an hour faster than the Fw 190 and could outmaneuver both. But its most important feature was its combat radius of more than 800 miles, which enabled the P-51B to escort American bombers to the heart of the Reich. The Mustang was joined over Germany by two other American escort fighters. One was the Republic Aviation Corporation's P-47C Thunderbolt, a powerful single-engined plane whose combat radius at about this time was increased to some 500 miles by the addition of drop fuel tanks. The other was the Lockheed P-38F Lightning, a twin-engined aircraft that could escort the bombers up to 700 miles with drop tanks.

When Mustangs were sighted over Hanover, more than 200 miles inside German-held territory, Göring refused to believe the report and reprimanded the station that issued it. But not long afterward General Galland himself, aloft to inspect Luftwaffe day-fighter operations, was chased all the way back to Berlin by four Mustangs. Now Göring had to believe it, and he well understood the gravity of this new development. The introduction of the American long-range escorts, he said, was nothing less than "a tragedy." And, for the Luftwaffe, so it proved to be. "No longer was it a case of their bombers having to run the gantlet of our fighters," one Luftwaffe pilot recalled, "but of our having to run the gantlet of both their bombers and their fighters."

At the same time the Americans were also building up their bomber strength to a prodigious level. By mid-February of 1944 the Eighth Air Force boasted some 2,500 bombers and 1,200 fighters; the Luftwaffe day-fighter force had also grown, but only to about 1,000 planes. On the 20th of that month the Americans exerted the full power of their newly expanded muscle by launching a six-day series of raids against the German aircraft industry. During this "Big Week" campaign, the new fighter escorts held American bomber losses to 6 per cent, while 355 Luftwaffe day fighters were destroyed and another 155 were damaged. In the wake of the Big Week disaster, the Germans reorganized and stepped up their production of fighter aircraft. Although Hitler still obstinately insisted that bombers should have priority, production of single-engined fighters rose from less than

900 aircraft a month in February to more than 2,000 in April.

But the heaviest cost of Big Week to the Luftwaffe day-fighter force was not in aircraft but in personnel; losses for the month of February totaled 225 men killed or missing and 141 more wounded—10 per cent of its active roster of fliers and air crewmen.

As the Americans maintained the pressure over the following months with daylight raids on Berlin and continued attacks on the aircraft industry, Luftwaffe personnel losses mounted alarmingly. Galland reported to Luftwaffe High Command at the end of April that since the beginning of 1944 his day-fighter force had lost more than 1,000 pilots. "They included our best Staffel, Gruppe and Geschwader commanders," he wrote, and warned: "The time has come when our force is within sight of collapse."

The Luftwaffe training command was turning out large numbers of fliers to meet the attrition, but to maintain quantity the training command had shortened its courses. Student pilots received only some 30 hours' flight time in single-engined fighters before being sent to operational units, down from 50 hours at the beginning of the War. And because the best fliers were needed for combat, instructors were generally poorly qualified. As a result the new aviators, many of them downy-cheeked teenagers, were ill prepared for the raging air war into which they were thrown. Many never even made it that far: In one hapless class for Me 109 pilots, 32 of 100 students died in crashes before finishing the course.

The Luftwaffe did not attempt to deal with the new American escort fighters through direct confrontation. Göring actually ordered his fliers to avoid the enemy fighters but to continue trying to bring down the bombers. This led to a growing confidence among the American fighter pilots, who soon made a practice of venturing beyond their escort duties to seek out and attack German fighters before they could get anywhere near the bombers. In effect, the Americans established command of the air over the German homeland.

Immediately after the June 6 Allied landings in France, British and American air power was temporarily focused on helping ground forces gain a secure foothold on the Continent. But within days the bombers and their fighter escorts were back over Germany—and over the oil fields of German-held Rumania—in a drive to destroy the German petroleum industry.

The attacks on oil fields, refineries and synthetic petroleum plants proved the most effective means the Allies had yet devised for strangling the Luftwaffe. The production of aviation fuel dropped from 195,000 tons in May to 35,000 tons in July and to only 7,000 tons in September. Stockpiled reserves kept the Luftwaffe flying at normal operational levels through the summer, but by fall shortages were acute—ironically, just at the time that the German aircraft-manufacturing industry hit a new peak in fighter production: 3,133 planes during September. Without sufficient fuel, the new aircraft were useless. To save fuel, pilot-training programs were curtailed further and sorties in support of ground forces at the fronts were cut to the minimum. Even the pilots of defensive-fighter units found themselves temporarily grounded between fuel deliveries, helplessly watching Allied bombers thunder overhead on their way to more raids on the oil industry.

In spite of the fuel shortage and Germany's apparently hopeless predicament, Hitler made a desperate attempt at the end of 1944 to rescue victory with an offensive operation. In mid-December German ground forces struck at the thin enemy lines in the Ardennes region of Belgium and drove a salient into Allied territory that gave its name to the battle that ensued: the Bulge. To provide air support for the Army, Göring diverted two thirds of the day-fighter force and a third of the night-fighter force from their defensive duties. Flying on fuel saved by cutting back all operations not immediately useful to the offensive, the pilots managed to make some 800 strafing and bombing runs a day. But Luftwaffe losses were high, and within two weeks it was evident that the advance had lost its momentum against stiffening Allied resistance.

Neither Hitler nor Göring was ready to call off the offensive, however, and on January 1, 1945, some 900 German planes were thrown into a surprise attack on Allied airfields in Belgium, Holland and France. The New Year's Day operation claimed about 200 Allied aircraft, but it proved to be a final paroxysm of offensive action for the Luftwaffe, which never recovered from its own losses that day. The Germans could easily replace the 300-odd planes that the operation cost them, but not the 253 pilots, including 19 Geschwader, Gruppe and Staffel commanders. In mid-January the Ardennes offensive ended in failure and the Allies again pressed their advance on the German homeland.

After the massive expenditure of precious fuel on the Ardennes operation, Luftwaffe fighter pilots found themselves grounded for longer and longer periods. One Gruppe supply officer who sent out tank trucks to find fuel said that it sometimes took him a week to collect enough for one operation. The idled pilots chafed. Many had made literally hundreds of combat sorties, and still they wanted to go on flying, impelled by patriotism, a desire to help protect loved ones and the sheer thrill of the dangerous game.

As the War worsened, the pilots became increasingly estranged from their leaders. They developed an esprit that made little allowance for headquarters nonsense and regulations. Their disaffection, in some cases, was blatant. Colonel Johannes Steinhoff, an ace who flew 993 missions, described the appearance of a fellow pilot, Major Erich Hohagen. Hohagen bore the marks of his valor; a crash had left him, after surgery, with a piece of plastic in his skull and a face whose two halves, as Steinhoff put it, "no longer quite matched."

"He wore a black cap of the kind students wear after a bad duel," Steinhoff said, "and it was pulled right down over his eyes, though

Bizarre aircraft born of desperation

During the waning days of the War, as Allied bombers pounded Germany relentlessly, the Reich's foremost aircraft designers rushed to develop new fighter-interceptors. The result was an odd assortment of unorthodox aircraft—from the Blohm und Voss 40 (below), a tiny glider that its pilot controlled while lying face down on the floor, to the Bachem 349 Natter, or "viper" (page 165), a futuristic and inexpensive rocket fighter that was constructed mainly of wood. In spite of the tense, round-the-clock efforts that were lavished on these aircraft, all of them were developed too late to reverse the Luftwaffe's—and Germany's—declining fortunes. Of the six shown here and on the following pages, only one, the Messerschmitt 163, ever saw combat. Although it achieved some success, too few Me 163s were produced to affect the outcome of the War.

The Blohm und Voss 40, a glider less than 19 feet long, was designed to dive into formations of Allied bombers at a maximum speed of 560 mph, then attack head on with its two 30-mm. cannon.

Boasting a 67-foot wingspan and a 1,610-hp engine, the Blohm und Voss 155 might have outperformed Allied fighters above 40,000 feet had not design problems hampered its development.

At 470 mph one of the fastest piston-engined fighters ever built, the Dornier 335 owed its speed to a second engine and propeller mounted aft of the tail.

Powered by the reaction of two highly volatile fuels, the 600-mph Messerschmitt 163 rocket fighter tended to explode during a rough landing.

The manned Bachem 349 rocket (right) was supposed to discharge the missiles in its nose, then crash while pilot and reusable engine drifted earthward by parachute.

With its rugged turbojet engine perched atop a simple metal fuselage, the Heinkel 162 was easy to mass-produce but challenging to fly.

some of the straw-colored hair still escaped. In defiance of every dress regulation (which we fighter pilots had in any case stopped observing long before) he had wound a fox fur round the collar of his yellow leather jacket (British booty—Dunkirk, probably). And he wore fur boots. The only 'regulation' parts of his rig were the bit of trouser leg visible (Luftwaffe blue) and the Knight's Cross pinned to the fox fur.'' Hohagen became so disgusted with the Luftwaffe's High Command that he renounced his Knight's Cross, but at the end of the War, when the Reich had already virtually ceased to exist, he was one of a small group of pilots who continued to fly sorties against the Allied bombers.

Despite the indisputable bravery of such men as Hohagen, Göring habitually referred to the Luftwaffe pilots as cowards and blamed them for the looming defeat. Once when a fighter operation failed, he ordered Galland to have one aviator from each fighter squadron "tried by courts martial for cowardice in the face of the enemy." Galland managed to persuade Göring to rescind the absurd order—but the bitter memory of the affair, and other demonstrations of the Reich Marshal's attitude, lingered, building in the hearts of the fliers a poisonous reservoir of resentment against their once-beloved Iron Man.

The truth was that Göring was using his men as scapegoats for the wrath that Hitler heaped upon him with increasing fury as Allied victories mounted. And just as Hitler became more and more difficult for Göring to reach, so did the Reich Marshal remove himself from close working contact with his subordinates, adding to their anger.

A group of disaffected pilots, including a few group commanders, tried to get Göring ousted from his post. Unbeknownst to them, their every move was watched and some of their telephones were tapped. They failed, but on the advice of the chief of the Luftwaffe general staff, Göring agreed to hear their grievances. The remarkable encoun-

The incongruous Mistel consisted of a scrapped Ju 88 bomber, packed with explosives, and an Fw 190 fighter. The Fw 190 flew the Ju 88 over target and dropped it like a bomb. Some 250 Mistels were put together between 1943 and 1945 for last-ditch Luftwaffe offensives.

A gallant ace and gifted debater, Colonel Günther Lützow was chosen by his fellow fighter pilots to present their grievances to an increasingly abusive Reich Marshal Hermann Göring in January of 1945. Livid at Lützow's temerity, Göring threatened to have him shot.

ter took place in January of 1945 at the Luftwaffe Club in Berlin.

Among the rebels was Colonel Steinhoff. As he waited for the meeting, Steinhoff recalled that Göring had once seemed to him "a figure of Wagnerian opera" who "conjured up before our eyes an almost tangible image of his new romantic ideal—the knight of the technological age." Now, as the Reich Marshal entered the room, Steinhoff was struck by the ironic contrast between that old image and Göring's present appearance: "It was a weary face, bloated and with folds like an old woman's falling from the mouth to the double chin, which in turn folded over the pale blue uniform collar encircling the massive neck. His flaccid skin showed traces of pink powder."

The pilots' spokesman, Colonel Günther Lützow, opened briskly, warning Göring with unprecedented temerity that if he interrupted, as he habitually did, the discussion would be pointless. Göring sat, Steinhoff recalled, "as if turned to stone," and listened as Lützow stated the pilots' case.

"Reich Marshal," he said, "your fighter pilots, particularly the day fighters, are extremely concerned about the immediate future of their service and their chances of playing an effective part in the defense of the Reich. We are aware that you, sir, come in for heavy criticism on account of the alleged failure of the fighter force. You for your part have had no hesitation in passing that criticism on to us by accusing us of 'loss of nerve' and even at times of cowardice. Your fighter force is still in a position to relieve the country by putting at least a temporary stop to the bomb terror. We believe, however, that this means concentrating all efforts on fighter operations as systematically as possible."

Lützow then got down to specifics. He called for strengthening the fighter units with "all available forces," including the Luftwaffe's bomber reserve, and employing them "in a concentrated fashion" under fighter force officers. Then he touched a subject that would be a sore point with the Führer as well as Göring.

After six years of secret development, the Messerschmitt company had brought into production the world's first operational military jet aircraft, the Messerschmitt 262. In addition to its unprecedented speed, up to 540 miles an hour, the new plane had the distinct advantage of burning low-octane diesel fuel, which was considerably more plentiful and easier to produce than the high-octane fuel that piston-driven planes consumed. One unit of more than 40 Me 262s, designated Jagdgeschwader 7, was already on operational fighter duty, but Hitler, still clinging to the notion that he could win the War with an air offensive, was determined that most of the new jets would be used as bombers. Göring could not be expected to rejoice as Lützow demanded "that all Me 262 jet aircraft be released immediately for fighter operations." Göring's beringed hand fell to the table with a slap, but Lützow continued. "There is still time, sir, to prevent every city in Germany from being reduced to rubble and ashes."

At last the Reich Marshal responded. "Your insolence in this matter positively defies belief," he declared icily. "You presume to dictate to me how I should be running my Luftwaffe. You are asking me to put everything in together, concentrate everything including my bombers. Well, that's exactly what I'm not going to do. I'd be a fool not to keep this powerful, magnificent reserve for the moment when I decide to strike the decisive blow. You want the Me 262 and you're not going to get it because I'm giving it to the people who know what to do with it, namely my bomber pilots."

Now Göring exploded. "What you're presenting me with here, gentlemen, is treason—mutiny! It's absolutely monstrous that you should conspire behind my back. I shall take appropriate action!" Pushing back his chair to rise, he bellowed at the pilots' spokesman, "Lützow, you . . . I'll have *you* shot!"

Lützow was not shot. Word of the pilots' rebellion reached the Führer, who ordered Göring to yield. "Give Galland a chance to prove that this aircraft is a superior fighter," Hitler said. "Give him a unit."

Thus was born, in the waning hours of the Reich, one of the most remarkable outfits in the history of military aviation, Jagdverband 44, which assembled at an air base near Munich. "It was clear to everyone," said Steinhoff, "that this airfield would be the end of the road as far as we were concerned." But meanwhile, there was still a war to fight. For his part, Galland had been itching to take an Me 262 into combat ever since he had first flown one on May 22, 1943, when he had felt "as though the angels were pushing." To fly with him in the new jets, he rounded up some 50 of the most raffish, battle-toughened veterans ever assembled, some of whom came directly from the Luftwaffe pilots' rest home, where they had been recovering from combat stress. "Many," said Galland, "reported without consent or transfer orders. Most of them had been in action since the first day of the War, and all of them had been wounded. All bore the scars of war and displayed the highest medals. The Knight's Cross was, so to speak, the badge of our unit. Now, after a long period of technical and numerical inferiority, they wanted once more to experience the feeling of air superiority. For this they were ready once more to chance sacrificing their lives."

The fliers did not find it easy to adjust to the new aircraft. Soon after the unit was formed, Steinhoff, who was in charge of teaching Galland's pilots the art of handling the Me 262, was flying one of the jets near the Eastern Front when he sighted a group of Soviet fighters. Carefully, he flattened out and headed for the Russians, the sun at his back so that they would be blinded by it. But he had not given enough allowance for the Me 262's great speed; in a split second what had been just black dots on the armored glass in front of his face became a swarm of fighter planes, and in another split second he had passed one "as if it was hanging motionless in the air." He felt a twinge of doubt: "Is this really such a good fighter?" Then, with a scant 25 minutes of flying time left,

Fighter ace Johannes Steinhoff, once called "the handsomest man in the Luftwaffe," perches jauntily on his Me 109 on the Eastern Front in 1942. Later he joined Adolf Galland's elite squadron, JV-44, flying the revolutionary Me 262 jets.

Horribly burned when his Me 262 crashed upon takeoff in the War's final days, Steinhoff wears an eye patch and protective glasses during his convalescence in a Munich hospital. He later became a key architect of Germany's postwar Luftwaffe.

Steinhoff saw a half dozen Soviet Shturmovik fighter-bombers strafing and bombing German infantry. He went into a steep diving turn, then leveled off above and behind the Russians.

"As I bent forward to look through the sight, I noticed that I had too much speed again. The trees and fields were flashing past beneath me and the shape of the last fighter-bomber loomed alarmingly in the sight." He repeated the instructions he often gave to his students: "Aim the luminous spot in the center of the sight at the middle of his fuselage, press the trigger by squeezing your hand round the stick, then pull the stick back sharply to avoid a collision." Carefully, Steinhoff followed his own instructions. "The burst of fire was very short," he said later. "The Shturmovik started leaving a trail just as I pulled up over it." Groaning as the Me 262's acceleration pushed him back against the seat, Steinhoff saw the Soviet plane crunch into the snow near the edge of the forest.

By the end of February 1945, the Allies were squeezing the life out of the Reich. The Soviets had advanced to the Oder River, within 50 miles of Berlin, and the Americans and British had reached the Rhine. Every day Galland's Me 262s—as well as Jagdgeschwader 7, the jet-fighter unit that had been formed the year before—went up against the enemy bombers that were, Steinhoff said, "like so many spiders drawing their vapor-trail threads across the gray blue sky." And, often, the missions scored.

"I was now lower than the bomber formation," Steinhoff recalled of one encounter, "and my speed was enormous. A Liberator floated through my sight, and the cannon spat a two- or three-second burst. My speed swung me up 2,000 or 3,000 meters above the bombers and I saw the Liberator I had attacked leaving a dark trail behind him. A hit!"

But Steinhoff saw too that the bomber formation continued on, and behind it came another. "We were like dayflies," he said, "who had come to the end of their day, where the dream dissolves into nothingness. Why did we still fly? Whom were we doing it for?" But whenever the order to take off came, Steinhoff hurried out to the flight line to check his machine, running a hand over the fuselage "the way one strokes a horse's neck." At such moments flying became enough reason in itself, and then "that curious feeling of power and superiority swept over me as it did every time I took off in the Me 262. The question why I flew, why I was a fighter pilot, simply receded into the background. The Americans had reached Crailsheim, the Russians were advancing on Berlin, and the Luftwaffe—apart from us—no longer existed. It was a dangerous kind of therapy I was using. Worse—it was an insane piece of self-deception."

On April 18, Steinhoff's plane malfunctioned and crashed as he attempted to take off to attack a raiding force of Flying Fortresses headed for Regensberg. He survived but was hideously burned in the crash. By now the German piston-engined fighters had virtually ceased operations. The Luftwaffe was disintegrating rapidly; some units were transferred into the Army and others simply disbanded. Only the jet pilots stubbornly continued flying. Göring and what was left of the Luftwaffe command retreated to Berchtesgaden in southern Germany.

On May 5, three days before Germany surrendered, the Reich Marshal was taken prisoner by American forces. Along with other German leaders, he was convicted a year later of war crimes by the Nuremberg tribunal and sentenced to death by hanging. Göring asked that he be shot instead, as befitted a soldier. When his request was refused, he swallowed a poison capsule that he had managed to conceal ever since his capture and died in his cell on October 15, 1946, two hours before his scheduled execution.

Some 265,000 members of the Luftwaffe had been killed or reported missing in action during the War. Another 213,000 had been wounded. Their achievement was great. When the War eventually turned against Germany they had fought on with devotion and skill, although they were "wrongly equipped and wrongly engaged," as Steinhoff put it. They destroyed some 70,000 enemy planes while losing 62,500 of their own. Their individual records surpassed those of any other air force: 103 Luftwaffe pilots had more than 100 kills each to their credit by the end of the War; 13 had more than 200, and two fliers, Erich Hartmann and Gerhard Barkhorn, had downed more than 300 enemy planes each. Most of the world condemned the cause the Luftwaffe fliers served, but few among their critics could find fault with the quality of their service.   ～

On May 9, 1945, one day after being taken prisoner, Hermann Göring undergoes a press conference in an Augsburg garden. When asked about his wartime boast that if the Allies ever bombed Berlin "My name is Meyer," the usually garrulous Göring reddened, mopped his face and said nothing.

Acknowledgments

The index for this book was prepared by Gale Linck Partoyan. For their valuable help in the preparation of this volume, the editors wish to thank: **In East Germany:** East Berlin—S. Hannes Quaschinsky, ADN, Zentralbild. **In France:** Paris—André Bénard, Odile Benoist, Elisabeth Bonhomme, Alain Degardin, George Delaleau, Gilbert Deloizy, Yvan Kayser, Général Pierre Lissarague, Director, Jean-Yves Lorent, Stéphane Nicolaou, Général Roger de Ruffray, Deputy Director, Colonel Pierre Willefert, Curator, Musée de l'Air; George Roland, E.C.P. Armées; Soignolles-en-Brie—Jean Cuny; Toulouse—Patrick P. Laureau; Vincennes—Marcellin Hodeir, S.H.A.A. **In Great Britain:** London—Group Captain Mieczyslaw Mumler, T. J. Krzystek, Secretary General, Polish Air Force Association in Great Britain; Worcester—Group Captain Aleksander K. Gabszewicz, President, Polish Air Force Association in Great Britain. **In the United States:** Washington, D.C.—Thomas T. Helde, Georgetown University; Alice Price, the Pentagon; C. Glenn Sweeting, National Air and Space Museum; John G. Ulrich, Chief, Defense Mapping Agency; New York—Colonel John R. Elting (Ret.); Ohio—Williamson Murray, Ohio State University; Oregon—Gordon W. Gilkey, Portland Art Museum; Virginia—Harris Andrews; Louis S. Casey; George Petersen. **In West Germany:** Altenberg—Günter Sengfelder; Babenhausen—Hans Novarra; Baden-Baden—General Hannes Trautloft (Ret.); Bonn—General Adolf Galland (Ret.), Roy Koch, Wanda Menke-Glückert, General Johannes Steinhoff (Ret.); Cologne—Gebhardt Aders, Captain Winfried Schmidt (Ret.); Koblenz—Meinrad Nilges, Marianne Loenartz, Bundesarchiv; Königsbrunn-Augsburg—Hanfried Schliephake; Captain Horst Amberg (Ret.), Gemeinschaft Der Jagdflieger; Hans Ebert, Messerschmitt-Bölkow-Blohm; Heinrich Graf von Einsiedel; Captain Otto Hintze (Ret.); Wolfgang Mayer; Munich—Dee Pattee; Günther Rall; Hans Ring; Mainz-Finthen—Karl Ries; Nuremberg—Captain Manfred Riegel (Ret.); Ransbach—Werner Held; Rösrath-Hoffnungsthal—Janusz Piekalkiewicz; Weil—Erich and Ursula Hartmann; West Berlin—Dr. Roland Klemig, Heidi Klein, Bildarchiv Preussischer Kulturbesitz, Wolfgang Streubel, Ullstein Bilderdienst.

Particularly useful sources of information and quotations used in this volume were: *The Luftwaffe War Diaries* by Cajus Bekker, Macdonald, London, 1966; *Battle Over the Reich* by Alfred Price, Ian Allan Ltd., London, 1973; and *Instruments of Darkness: The History of Electronic Warfare* by Alfred Price, Chas. Scribner's Sons, 1977.

Bibliography

Books

Aders, Gebhard, *History of the German Night Fighter Force 1917-1945*. London: Jane's Publishing Company, 1979.

Baldwin, Hanson, *Battles Lost and Won*. Harper & Row, 1966.

Bekker, Cajus, *The Luftwaffe War Diaries*. London: Macdonald, 1966.

Carell, Paul, *The Foxes of the Desert*. E. P. Dutton, 1961.

Collier, Richard:
The City That Would Not Die: The Bombing of London, May 10-11, 1941. E. P. Dutton, 1960.
Eagle Day: The Battle of Britain, August 6-September 15, 1940. E. P. Dutton, 1980.

Constable, Trevor J., and Raymond F. Toliver, *Horrido! Fighter Aces of the Luftwaffe*. Macmillan, 1968.

Deighton, Len, *Fighter—The True Story of the Battle of Britain*. Alfred A. Knopf, 1978.

Esposito, Vincent J., *The West Point Atlas of American Wars, Vol. 2, 1900-1953*. Frederick A. Praeger, 1959.

Galland, Adolf, *The First and the Last: The Rise and Fall of the German Fighter Forces, 1938-1945*. Henry Holt, 1954.

Hartmann, Erich, *Der Jagdflieger*. Stuttgart: Motorbuch Verlag, 1978.

Horne, Alistair, *To Lose a Battle, France 1940*. Little, Brown, 1969.

Jablonski, Edward, *Terror from the Sky*. Doubleday, 1971.

Mason, Herbert Molloy, Jr., *The Rise of the Luftwaffe: Forging the Secret German Weapon, 1918-1940*. Dial Press, 1973.

Middlebrook, Martin, *The Nuremberg Raid, 30-31 March 1944*. William Morrow, 1974.

Mosley, Leonard, and the Editors of Time-Life Books, *The Battle of Britain*. Time-Life Books, 1977.

Obermaier, Ernst, *Die Ritterkreuzträger der Luftwaffe: Jagdflier 1939-1945*. Mainz, Germany: Verlag Dieter Hoffmann, 1966.

Parkinson, Roger, *Summer, 1940: The Battle of Britain*. David McKay, 1977.

Plocher, Hermann, *The German Air Force Versus Russia, 1942*. Arno Press, 1966.

Price, Alfred:
Battle Over the Reich. London: Ian Allan, 1973.
Luftwaffe: Birth, life and death of an air force. London: Macdonald, 1970.

Rudel, Hans-Ulrich, *Stuka Pilot*. Dublin: Euphorion Books, 1953.

Sims, Edward H., *The Greatest Aces*. Ballantine Books, 1967.

Smith, Peter C., *Stuka at War*. Scribner's, 1980.

Snyder, Louis L., *Encyclopedia of the Third Reich*. McGraw-Hill, 1976.

Steinhoff, Johannes, *The Last Chance: The Pilots' Plot Against Göring, 1944-1945*. London: Hutchinson, 1977.

Tantum, W. H., IV, and E. J. Hoffschmidt, *The Rise and Fall of the German Air Force (1933 to 1945)*. WE Inc., 1969.

Toliver, Raymond F., and Trevor J. Constable:
The Blond Knight of Germany. Doubleday, 1970.
Fighter Aces of the Luftwaffe. Aero, 1977.

Townsend, Peter, *Duel of Eagles*. Simon and Schuster, 1970.

Wernick, Robert, and the Editors of Time-Life Books, *Blitzkrieg*. Time-Life Books, 1976.

Wood, Tony, and Bill Gunston, *Hitler's Luftwaffe: A pictorial history and technical encyclopedia of Hitler's air power in World War II*. Crescent Books, no date.

Ziemke, Earl F., *The German Northern Theater of Operations, 1940-1945*. U.S. Government Printing Office, 1959.

Picture credits

The sources for the illustrations are listed below. Credits from left to right are separated by semicolons, from top to bottom by dashes.
Endpaper (and cover detail, regular edition): Painting by Richard Schlecht. 6, 7: Süddeutscher Verlag Bilderdienst, Munich. 8, 9: Courtesy Hanfried Schliephake, Königsbrunn/Augsburg, Federal Republic of Germany; Bundesarchiv, Koblenz. 10, 11: Karl Ries, Mainz-Finthen, Federal Republic of Germany; courtesy Hanfried Schliephake, Königsbrunn/Augsburg, Federal Republic of Germany. 12, 13: Ullstein Bilderdienst, Berlin (West). 14, 15: Courtesy Gebhard Aders, Cologne. 16: Bundesarchiv, Koblenz. 17, 18: Ullstein Bilderdienst, Berlin (West). 19: Polish Photo Agency, Warsaw. 21: Courtesy Janusz Piekalkiewicz, Rösrath-Hoffnungsthal, Federal Republic of Germany. 23, 25: Bundesarchiv, Koblenz. 27: Courtesy collection of George Petersen. 30: ADN Zentralbild, Berlin (DDR). 32, 33: Courtesy Embassy of the Polish People's Republic and Edward Jablonski. 35: Wide World. 36-41: Drawings by John Batchelor. 42: Bildarchiv Preussischer Kulturbesitz, Berlin (West). 44: Photo Reporters, Inc. 45: UPI. 48: Courtesy Janusz Piekalkiewicz, Rösrath-Hoffnungsthal, Federal Republic of Germany. 51: From *Der Adler*, 1940, courtesy University Library, Mannheim, Foto Norbert Nordmann, Bonn. 55: USAF, Albert F. Simpson Historical Research Center. 57: Imperial War Museum, London—courtesy Gebhard Aders, Cologne—Bundesarchiv, Koblenz. 59, 61: Imperial War Museum, London. 62: Courtesy Janusz Piekalkiewicz, Rösrath-Hoffnungsthal, Federal Republic of Germany. 66-69: Bundesarchiv, Koblenz. 70, 71: Bundesarchiv, Koblenz—collection of Wolfgang Mayer, Munich; Bildarchiv Preussischer Kulturbesitz, Berlin (West). 72, 73: From *Der Adler*, 1940, courtesy University Library, Mannheim, Foto Norbert Nordmann, Bonn; Bildarchiv Preussischer Kulturbesitz, Berlin (West). 74, 75: Bildarchiv Preussischer Kulturbesitz, Berlin (West)—National Archives No. 131-NO-7-36; Bundesarchiv, Koblenz. 76, 77: Courtesy collection of George Petersen. 80: Wide World. 84: Drawing

by Frederic F. Bigio from B-C Graphics. 85: Drawing by John Batchelor. 87: Courtesy Karl Ries, Mainz-Finthen, Federal Republic of Germany. 89, 91: From *Signal* magazine, courtesy George Petersen. 93: Bundesarchiv, Koblenz. 94: Imperial War Museum, London—Bernhard Jope, Butzbach, Federal Republic of Germany; courtesy collection of George Petersen. 97: Bundesarchiv, Koblenz (2); Wide World. 98, 99: Culver Pictures. 100, 101: *ME-109's and a Wellington Bomber Formation* by H. Recksiegel, courtesy U.S. Air Force Art Collection. 102: *Stuka Attack on an English Harbor* by H. Recksiegel, courtesy U.S. Air Force Art Collection. 103: *Sunderland Bomber Attacked by a Fighter* by H. Recksiegel, courtesy U.S. Air Force Art Collection. 104, 105: *German Bombers Over London* by Julius Schmitz-Westerholt, courtesy U.S. Air Force Art Collection. 106, 107: Courtesy Karl Ries, Mainz-Finthen, Federal Republic of Germany. 108: Map by Tarijy Elsab. 110: From *Signal* magazine, courtesy George Petersen. 113: UPI. 114: Wide World. 118: Courtesy Werner Held, Ransbach-Baumbach, Federal Republic of Germany. 119: Bundesarchiv, Koblenz. 120, 121: Margaret Bourke-White for *Life.* 123-127: Bundesarchiv, Koblenz. 128: UPI. 129: Courtesy Hanfried Schliephake, Königsbrunn/Augsburg, Federal Republic of Germany. 130, 131: Novosti Press Agency, London. 132-139: Archiv Erich Hartmann, Weil, Federal Republic of Germany. 140-143: Bundesarchiv, Koblenz. 144, 145: Courtesy collection of George Petersen; courtesy Gunther Heise, Munich—from *Instruments of Darkness: The History of Electronic Warfare,* © 1967, 1977, Alfred Price, published by Charles Scribner's Sons and Jane's Publishing Ltd., London; Ullstein Bilderdienst, Berlin (West). 147-151: Drawings by John Batchelor. 152, 153: Courtesy collection of George Petersen. 155: Imperial War Museum, London. 156: Ullstein Bilderdienst, Berlin (West). 158, 159: USAF, courtesy Alfred Price, Uppingham, Leicestershire, England. 163: MBB, Hamburg. 164: Smithsonian Institution Neg. No. 72-8522—ADN Zentralbild, Berlin (DDR)—Smithsonian Institution Neg. No. A435416. 165: Smithsonian Institution Neg. No. 80-14838. 166: Imperial War Museum, London. 167, 168: Bundesarchiv, Koblenz. 169: Foto Norbert Nordmann, courtesy Johannes Steinhoff, Bonn. 171: Margaret Bourke-White for *Life.*

Index